Turning Points:

Action Today, Change Tomorrow

Richard Osibanjo

WestBow Press books may be ordered through booksellers or by contacting:

WestBow Press
A Division of Thomas Nelson
1663 Liberty Drive
Bloomington, IN 47403
www.westbowpress.com
1-(866) 928-1240

ISBN: 978-1-4497-5608-6 (sc)
ISBN: 978-1-4497-5609-3 (e)

Printed in the United States of America

WestBow Press rev. date:12/12/2012

In loving memory of my mother

Titilayo Olayinka Osibanjo

For loving and teaching me by an exemplary life

Contents

Failure and Success in Life

Foreword

It has been my privilege to pastor and to get to know Richard Osibanjo over the last three years. Richard has an amazing passion for Jesus, a love for the local church, a thirst for knowledge, and a brilliant gift of communication. This book reflects some of his attitudes, meditations, and thoughts that are enabling him to become a world-class leader. Almost all of our decisions and attitudes in life are the result of "seed thoughts" and mind-sets that have been hibernating and germinating in our minds. Those thoughts and attitudes eventually become conversations that direct our actions and set the course for our destiny. So the seeds I plant in my mind every day, although they may look small and insignificant at the time, end up determining the trajectory of my life. In his book *Turning Points,* Richard gives us daily devotionals, or "seed thoughts," that can shape the way we think and have a powerful impact on our decisions for the future. I highly recommend using this book as a daily devotional, along with your Bible reading and other books, to help shape your mind and give you a fresh perspective. Each chapter contains a key thought that will stick with you and help to transform your mind with practical wisdom you won't forget.

David Patterson
Lead Pastor
The Father's House
Vacaville CA

Preface

I was hanging out with Tom, a very good friend of mine, when he revisited a childhood story he had told me. Tom had moved at least seventeen times and lived in dire conditions by the time he was twelve. One of those instances involved him and his family camping around a lake for six months because they had no place to live. Ironically, that was one of his favorite memories growing up because the experience bonded his family together. Tom also recalled seeing drugs in the house when he was eight and had experienced several things that no child his age should have.

But despite his unusual childhood, his mum ensured him that he would never miss school, for which he was grateful. According to Tom, school was the only place he felt normal. He was determined to break the cycle of poverty in his family, and fortunately for him, he excelled in his studies. Tom admitted he was a troubled child and needed help, so his way of getting noticed at school was being the best. His academic excellence endeared him to his teachers, who became an invaluable resource to him through mentoring. Today, Tom is successful and works at a Fortune 500 company. Yet despite his success, Tom is very humble and takes his relationships with his family seriously.

Unfortunately, not every story like Tom's has a happy ending. Many of Tom's siblings, due to no fault of their own, became victims of the cycle they were born into. It was difficult for them to aspire to a better world than they had ever experienced. Tom's story, like many "American greats," inspires my writing and proves that our background does not have to determine our foreground. Failure, like success, is a choice, and only you can make that decision. Although Tom had a troubled childhood, he chose to break the cycle through his daily decisions and actions. He had a mental picture of where he wanted to be, and that fueled his passion.

I do not know your story or what you are going through, but one thing I know for certain is there are many Toms out there. You cannot do anything about the past, but you can rewrite your future. I hope this book helps you in your journey to becoming the star you were designed to be. I encourage you to take one step at a time and pick yourself back up when you fall. Your dream future is just a day away, and you will surely reach your destination. As in any performance, it is the exit that is often remembered. There is hope for you.

Acknowledgments

I remember the day at The Father's House in Vacaville, California, during our midweek service when I had a divine reminder to live my dream of writing, which I had abandoned for almost twenty years. I am grateful to God for the inspiration and guidance. I have not looked back since.

I would like to thank many people who have poured spiritual wisdom into my life, especially Pastors Titus Olayinka, Akin and Eno Oluwole, and Dave Patterson, whose exemplary leadership have been an inspiration to me.

I also thank all the great authors and speakers whose books and audio messages have helped shape my life. These mentors have contributed greatly to my continuing education, and I thank each of them for their investment in me.

Special thanks to Carol Belleau and my aunties, Taiwo Owoeye and Peju Odunsi, who meticulously went through my writing and put things in proper perspective; to Arthur Thibert, Jon Ford, Michael Pinter, Gbenga Oshokoya, Gabriel Onagoruwa, Gavin Banks, Ethan Ostrom, and Chris Riedell for reviewing my book; to my best friend, Olutayo Osunkunle, for his support; to Brock Bennett, who inspired my choice of the book title and whose invaluable suggestions made a huge difference; to my "big brother" Dr. Ademola Idowu, who always inspires and believes in me; and to my cousins, Anne Aworinde and Korede Fadojutimi, who are simply the best.

Many thanks to my Father's House Friday small group, especially Peter Fredsholm and Andrew Travers, and to my group leaders, Geoff and Carol Belleau, for making a difference in our lives.

To my darling wife, who has been a pillar of support and encouragement throughout this process, I say a special thank you. You lovingly took care of our son, David, so I could write this book. I love you dearly. I am eternally grateful to my parents, Professor Oladele and Olusola Osibanjo, whose love and devotion have made a significant contribution to the person I am today. Special thanks to my sister Kemmy Lawson, whose passion for excellence inspires me, and to my brother, Olawale Osibanjo.

Relationships: Family, Friends, and Faith

There Is No Recipe for a Happy Relationship

The term *happy relationship* is relative. The criteria for judging whether a relationship is good or bad changes from person to person, which is why it is important you and your loved one work out what happy looks like to each of you in your relationship.

While I believe there is no recipe for a happy relationship, there are some ingredients that are always present in happy ones. Topping the list are unconditional love, respect, and forgiveness. Great relationships are never contractual. A relationship based on eye-for-an-eye, tooth-for-a-tooth is sure to fail.

There are many available resources for successful relationships, much of which can be confusing since people offer conflicting information on similar situations. In my experience, outside resources should serve as guides and not rules. No one knows your situation like you do. Although situations may be similar, people are different and they respond as such. Knowledge is powerful when it is applied, so I gather all the resources available to me and ask myself how I can apply them to my circumstance because there is no recipe. You must customize the information available to you and make it your own.

What does a happy relationship look like for your partner and you? Remember, it all starts in the mind. A future you cannot picture you cannot feature in. You may need to discuss with your partner what a happy relationship looks like to each of you and make a road map. It is okay if you are not there yet; you can determine in which direction you need to be headed.

Regardless of your relationship health status, you can start your journey by creating a picture of a happy relationship in your mind. As Napoleon Hill says, "Whatever your mind can believe and conceive, it can achieve."

Nobody Can Make You 100 Percent Happy

I was stuck in the pit of always outsourcing my happiness. I allowed other people to determine my contentment until I discovered that happiness was a gift from God to share *with* others and not derive *from* them.

Nobody can make you happy all the time. People's emotions are like butterflies, one minute up and the other down. I got tired from feeling I had done something wrong when someone around me was not happy. I finally realized I didn't need anyone to treat me a certain way to feel special.

Affirmations are great, but it is important you do not feel less valued when they are absent. My turning point came when I took responsibility for my happiness. I made sure what I thought and felt about myself were independent of other people's reactions to or perceptions of me. I became truly free from letting others define how I felt about myself. This new state of mind was really empowering and moved me from being a receiver to a giver. Being myself enabled others be themselves around me.

The definition of happiness and what makes us happy is a controversial subject. While it is true that material things and money can give us temporary happiness, the Journal Science, published an article that showed spending money on others made people happier than spending it on themselves[1]. I do not believe this concept is limited to only money or material things. You can give people a smile, touch, kindness, compliments, words, a listening ear, time—the list could be endless. The concept here is, happy people love to give. Why not make a list of the various ways you can be a blessing to others and then act on it? Happiness is a gift you share with other people.

True Riches

In the world today, you are considered wealthy based on how many material possessions you can acquire. There is nothing wrong with that if you have worked hard for them. However, the real question is, what has all this wealth and popularity cost?

Imagine you have one day left on earth. How will you spend it? I am guessing you will not want to be at the office or looking at your bank accounts. I believe you would want to spend that day with your friends and family, the people who mean the world to you. The truth is, all your accolades will not matter on that day. You cannot take them with you to the grave, and you don't know how your estate will be taken care of after you are gone. That being the case, your loved ones are your true riches.

Money and material things can be lost and replaced, but the loss of a loved one is final. So how much quality time are you devoting to your true riches on your road to success?

Relationships Are Dynamic, Never Static

Railroad tracks are usually made of iron and lay back to back for miles. An observer may not notice the occasional gaps between the tracks, which allow for the iron to expand when it is hot and to contract when it is cool. Without these gaps, the tracks would get distorted from the lack of room for the iron to shift, which would obviously be dangerous to travelers.

Like the railroad track, people's values and interests change with time, and it is important to give the people in your life room to grow. This helps to establish and build healthy relationships.

Black Is the Best Friendship Color

Can you imagine living in a world with only one color? It would be miserable and boring. Colors enrich and add beauty to our lives. They also have meanings associated with them, which depends on the context or environment. For example, colors can represent white for peace, green for the environment or nature, red for love or danger, and black for cool, evil, dark, or mysterious. But black is one of the controversial colors. Some cultures even associate black with mourning and often do not encourage the wearing of black outfits.

Colors can also define how we view our interpersonal relationships. In my experience, outgoing personalities are comfortable wearing bright colors while more introverted personalities prefer neutral or dull colors. I once had an interesting experience in a bike shop. I noticed the attendant was extra cautious with my bike, and I became uncomfortable because I wondered if there was something wrong. I watched how he handled other bikes, and the care was nothing compared to that which he gave mine. Later, the reason behind his actions became obvious. My handlebars and bike seat were white, so he was being very careful not to stain them. This observation got me wondering how colors can relate to interpersonal relationships.

Imagine dressing for work in a white outfit. I am sure you would be extra careful while drinking coffee, eating breakfast, or going about your daily routine to ensure you do not stain your outfit. Your sensitivity would be at its highest peak. A white outfit looks great, but it requires a lot of maintenance. Now imagine how your behavior would be different if you wore a black or dark-colored outfit. My guess is you would be more relaxed and not as careful.

In a similar way, I believe in making, having, and keeping friends, you may want to consider not wearing white in these relationships, as a white outfit could symbolize perfection, intolerance, lack of accommodation, and touchiness. Since we all have issues, when connecting with others, they could stain your "whiteness." Also, people may then be very cautious and uncomfortable around you. In my opinion, no one wants to be around such people for too long.

Black, however, is cool and more forgiving when it comes to hiding stains. In relationships, this could symbolize understanding, forgiveness, patience, and listening. I am sure you wouldn't feel as uncomfortable if a glass of red wine was spilled on your black outfit as you would on your white one.

What is your friendship color? How does that play out in your relationships?

Good Friends Are Like the Moon

Stars are never seen during the day, but they are always there. They shine brightest when it is pitch dark. Such are true friends—you may not see or hear from them all of the time, but they always show up when it matters, in that hour of need.

A kind person ran up to me the other day to give me my wallet, which had dropped from my pocket. I was so thankful because I imagined all the trouble and pain I would have gone through if I had lost it. This is the same feeling of comfort I get from my friends and family in my dark, down times. They always remind me that my trials are punctuations and not periods.

Great friends remind you that life is like a football match and your trials are the half times. You can have your opportunity at life again. Believe in yourself, and pitch your tent with people who believe in and want the best for you. Get connected with your old friends again, as no one knows you like they do. They are like warm blankets when the world grows cold.

Always Leave Two Doors Open: the Entrance and the Exit

Love is a gift, not a right, so when it starts sounding like one, its whole essence is lost. You cannot force anyone to love you or to stay with you, and honestly, you shouldn't need to. Your true friends will stay with you, rain or shine.

Trying to put a square peg in a round hole causes more pain, and it is not worth it. I have tried in the past to keep some relationships going even when the signs that they needed to end were obvious. In the process, I lost myself. I became someone I wasn't just to keep those people in my life. Any relationship that requires you to become someone else in order to be recognized is not worth it.

My best friends love me for being myself, and hanging out with them makes me a better person. I do not need to fit a particular description to be their friend.

Great relationships are not like some jobs, which are tasking; great relationships are voluntary and bring relief. Your true friends are in your life because they love you and want to be around you.

There is no fear in love. You should be accepted and celebrated for who you are. Your real friends are still out there. Discover who they are.

Allow Metamorphosis in Your Relationships

Metamorphosis is when innovation, growth, and transformation occur, resulting in a different outlook on life. Have you noticed that stores keep moving things around all the time? This is because they want their customers to spend a longer time in the store, increasing the possibility that they will see newer products and spend more money.

Predictability can lead to stagnation in relationships. To move forward, you may need to try new activities or do the old things in a different way. When my wife and I felt like we were acting like an old couple in our second year of marriage, we decided to do something about it. We had a date night every week and had friends over for a game night during the week. That worked for us, but we continually looked for other ways to keep our relationship interesting.

Hanging out with the same people day in and day out will eventually take its toll. You soon feel bored and start looking for a new adventure. An adventurous attitude is good for your mind, body, and relationships. This excitement will bring some zest into your life and can save what was becoming ordinary and boring.

Are You Needy or Loving?

If you want people to enjoy your company, you must enjoy your own company. Do not mistake the desire to be with people to needing people. Needy people constantly demand things, such as affirmation, time, attention, and resources. These characteristics are present in healthy, loving relationships, but when they become an obligation, the relationship dynamic changes and becomes unhealthy. The clingy person is usually an energy drain, so people avoid them.

Don't get me wrong—we all are needy at certain points or in certain situations in our lives. There were times in my life when I needed support and reassurance from my loved ones, and there is nothing wrong with that. It only becomes a problem when it is continuous. We all have needs, but we cannot allow our desires to control us. In fact, being needy will create a distance between you and your loved ones. Loving relationships are based on each party giving their best in the relationship and striving to be a blessing to others.

Being needy is a symptom of a bigger issue—self-esteem. You do not need anyone to treat you in a particular way to feel special. You are the only person who can do that. It is important that you are comfortable being yourself and allow others to do so as well, which is how healthy, long-lasting relationships are developed. So let your relationships develop naturally, and have a network of friends so you do not become overly dependent on any one person.

Be Patient with People

As a teenager, I lost my temper often and burned many bridges. I was never violent, but I hated the aftermath of my actions. I had to apologize to the people concerned for overreacting, as my behavior shifted attention from the main issue.

My best friend Tayo always told me to never close the door of a relationship in the heat of the moment. He said it was the easiest thing to do and could lead to a habit in other areas of my life in the future. I have since embarked on the journey of patience by putting myself in other people's shoes. It has not been easy, but I am making progress.

Adults, like babies, are not born with self-control. It is a skill learned over time. Patience is hard, a trait we expect *from* other people but forget to give *to* them. Patience is also a virtue. In relationships, the slow-and-steady person wins the hearts and minds of his or her loved ones. Patience helps us bear difficult situations and people without flying off the handle.

I have learned that there is great gain in remaining calm and collected instead of being impulsive. This can save your job, relationships, and life. It has saved mine, so give it a shot.

Remember: Love People and Use Things

The golden rule says, "Treat people the way you want to be treated." People are valuable and are your greatest assets. They are not just a number or a transaction or something you use to get what you want.

How do you know when you are using people and loving things? You know when you put yourself in their place, ask, "Is this the way I would want to be treated if I were in their shoes?", and the answer is no. Check your motives, and consider the other person's interests when you make decisions. Strive to ensure that everybody wins.

It is often difficult to tell initially if someone is using you or loving you, but time reveals deception. However, it is not in your best interests to be too guarded from being taken advantage of either. While someone may have used you, that experience may have made you stronger, wiser, and better. According to Massachuttes Institute of Technology's Brain and Cognitive Science department, studies have shown that we learn more from our failures than our successes[2].

Changing Seasons of Relationships

My best friend and I have come a long way, but one thing has remained constant, and that is change. Both of us at one point or another have changed some perspective on life, but we have learned to give each other room to grow without clinging to what was in the past. This has helped keep our friendship strong.

Similarly, the values and interests of your loved ones are constantly changing. It is good to stay connected and know what's going on in their lives. That way, you remain connected to who they were and with who they have become.

Team Player or Lone Ranger?

Being part of a team does not mean losing your individuality or originality. A true team player is also a lone ranger who knows that in order to be effective on the team, he has a responsibility to prepare and develop his own skills. Only when his skills are honed do they benefit the team.

When each team member does his part, it is easier to work together as a team to achieve a greater goal. The ideal team player knows when to play each role. A team is only as strong as its weakest link.

Some Doors Are Better Left Closed

Have you ever tried unlocking a door only to discover you had made a mistake? It was embarrassing, wasn't it? I was at the mall the other day, and I saw a car that looked like mine. I did everything I could to get into the car but later discovered from the license plates that I had made an error. I was frustrated, annoyed, and relieved at the same time. Those feelings reminded me of negative relationships I have had in the past. The more I tried to make things work, the more frustrated I became. I could never do enough to satisfy the other person. My passion had blinded me from looking at these relationships objectively, and the result was that they ended on a sad note.

It is okay to try to open a relationship door, but it is not okay to force one open. If you do, you will have to keep fighting to keep the relationship going. One-sided relationships are painful and frustrating, so you should have a great reason to be in one, as they usually drain your energy and resources. Relationships with spouses, family members, and other loved ones may require your persistence, regardless of their feedback.

It is vital you spend time with people who see your value and believe the best about you. Spending time with people who act as if they are doing you a favor only crushes your self-esteem. It is possible you may not have met your best friends yet, those who recognize your worth and treat you as such. Great relationships are worth waiting for.

Family Ties and Times Are Precious

Family is Gods gift to us; we can choose our friends but not our families. Family prepares us for the outside world. It is where our individuality is molded. Family life is like a rose—it has awesome beauty, but its thorns remind us there can be tough times too.

It is a child that opens his arms that can be carried.—Nigerian Proverb

I always look forward to seeing my fourteen-month-old son every evening when I get home from work. The first thing he does when he sees me is open his arms wide so I can pick him up with an expression that tells me he has missed me. My son is not afraid to show his vulnerability, which triggers an automatic response within me to cuddle him.

This concept can be applied to anyone who wants to be carried spiritually, mentally, emotionally, and physically. The people in your life are not mind readers. You need to take the risk of vulnerability so people can be a blessing to you. Trying to appear perfect only alienates you from your loved ones. We all fear being rejected—that's okay as long as we do not let it control us.

There are many mean people in this world but there are many more kind-hearted and loving people. It is important to be receptive and inviting by opening your heart to others. You are not telling someone you are happy to see him when you have a frown on your face or when your body language says otherwise.

Your vulnerability is what makes you human; accept it and be proud of it. So open your arms. There is someone waiting to lift you up.

Business Talk versus Relationship Talk

In America, people spend an average of fifty weeks a year at work, and so they are used to speaking from a business frame of mind. When speaking to your boss during a meeting, you typically give the main points or highlights of your report. But this method does not work well for all relationships. It is okay to give a *report* at work, but people want rappor*t* when speaking on a personal level.

Presents Should Not Replace Presence

I grew up always wishing my dad had just a bit more time for me. I received everything I asked for except his time, and this was so hurtful. My dad felt that as long as he was giving me what I needed, it was love at its best. While I was happy and grateful with the presents, I felt empty. I would rather have had his time and the presents be the icing on the cake.

My breakthrough came when I realized my dad only felt love through his work, as that was the one thing in his life that had never disappointed him. His dad was poor, and my dad's way out of poverty was by selling out to his work. When it finally dawned on me that I was asking for something he could not give, I could then move on.

My mom did a great job trying to fill the void, and I was blessed to have her in my life. I believe every child needs his or her parents' full participation in his or her life. A mother cannot fulfill the role of a father, and a father cannot fulfill the role of a mother. However, there are situations when it is unavoidable, and that is when other family members can step in and take more responsibility.

The best gift you can give your family is your presence. Nothing else comes close. You have something to offer your children no one else can. Your stories and past experiences can equip and empower them for the challenges ahead.

Be on the Same Page

To be successful in interpersonal relationships, both parties must be on the same page. Have you ever been in a relationship where you saw someone as a dear friend, but he or she saw you as something more? This is a tricky situation because it has the potential to destroy whatever relationship you have with one another.

Before you make assumptions about the chemistry between you and another person and dive into a relationship, make sure you find out what their expectations are for the relationship. You will be saving yourself a whole lot of heartache in the end. For two people to stay, play, and work together, they must be on the same page.

A Well-Watered Garden

Many people have said that healthy relationships are like a well-watered garden. I have found that a garden requires a lot of work, from tilling the ground, adding nutrients, planting, and watering. A garden, at least a beautiful one, is not a one-time affair; it requires regular maintenance to ensure the plants grow and blossom. A healthy plant is dependent on the soil and its nutrients and the climate. Some plants do better in the shade and some do better in full sun. It is important that everything is in the right order for the plant to thrive. A plant in an unsuitable environment will grow all right, but it will be stunted and may eventually develop a disease. Likewise, great relationships do not happen by chance; you have to work hard to nurture, maintain and keep them.

You Find Whatever You Are Looking For

You will find whatever you are looking for in people. A dog always lives up to its name. I have often wondered how the most obnoxious, recalcitrant, and sadistic people could have been in loving relationships. My only guess is that his or her loved ones must have seen something in them the world missed.

Many people are quick to label others. The problem with this is labels eventually define the person in our minds, and so they become whatever label we have placed on them. A label does account for people changing. We use one aspect of a person to define the whole person. We make quick positive or negative judgments about people and then look for evidence to support our theory. It is important to look for facts, not what we have imagined. Observe people holistically; get to know them before assigning any grade.

A good way to use a label is when you say positive things to people. For example, when you tell a loved one that he or she is the most caring person you have ever met, you will see that he or she will strive to live up to that label. Likewise, when you tell someone that he or she is no good, the person stops trying and becomes what you have labeled him or her.

Catch people doing the right things, and praise them for it. This has more power than doing the opposite.

Relationship Cycles

My childhood memories are precious to me considering how times have changed. I remember running down the street with my friends, flying kites, and having the time of our lives. Such times now seem like a luxury due to the crime rate and evolving times and seasons. My best memories are those in which I spent time with my friends, which made my life and world a better place. But over the course of time, some of my rock-solid relationships vaporized.

It is a sad truth, but some people will walk out of your life for no apparent reason, and some friends will be lost due to distance or changing interests. These things happen not because there is something wrong with you, but rather it is just a simple fact of life. Twenty children cannot play together for twenty years. It would be a shame to miss out on the time you could have with someone because of the pain of separation.

I have learned to celebrate and enjoy the relationships in my life at every season, so I leave very little room for regrets.

Give unto Caesar What Belongs to Caesar…Mark 12:17

As an extrovert, I enjoy meeting people on a daily basis. I realized with my ever-expanding social circle I was building a network but a lot of these relationships lacked depth. Now there is nothing wrong with having acquaintances, but it is important for balance to have a deep connection with close friends. Someone once said the path to friendship could easily be overgrown with weeds, so when treading that path, it is important to keep the path clear. Your old friends and new acquaintances should not compete for your time. Old friends have proven themselves, so they deserve your loyalty and time.

Abra-ca-hula

Imagine asking for directions in a foreign country where no one understands you. You would have a hard time locating your destination. Likewise, in relationships when you do not understand each other's love language, it leads to confusion, frustration, and even breakdown in communication.

Your love language is your personal way of expressing and interpreting love. Gary Chapman, a marriage counselor for over thirty years and a *New York Times* best-selling author, wrote the book *The Five Love Languages*. In it, he identifies the major love languages as words of affirmation, quality time, acts of service, physical touch, and giving of gifts. This book changed my life and the quality of my relationships. It is a must-read for anyone wanting to take his or her relationships to another level.

Do you know which love languages your loved ones speak? It is important you do so you can save yourself the frustration and ensure that your intentions are not perceived wrongly. Communication is the foundation of solid relationships, and understanding your loved ones' love language will give you a head start.

A love language is not about you but about the other person. By learning them, each party does those things that bring out the best in the other person. I learned this lesson the hard way. I thought the only way to show love was through how I felt loved and believed that people who didn't share my love-view were weird. My turning point came when a good friend of mine wanted to end our relationship. This experience taught me to wear different hats for different people in my life.

When I turned thirty, my wife had a surprise birthday party for me, but when she turned thirty, she was emphatic that a party was the last thing she wanted. I am an extrovert, so I really enjoyed the party she organized for me and assumed that my organizing a surprise birthday party for her would make her day. After all, it was good to reciprocate, right? Wrong. It is good to reciprocate a kind gesture but not necessarily the *same* gesture. Love people how they want to be loved and not how you think they should be loved.

You might wonder if loving someone the way they want to be loved requires your not being yourself. Relationships are give and take, and love is being able to accommodate others. I suggest that both parties be flexible enough where it does not hurt them or change who they are.

It is important that you communicate your expectations to your loved ones. Where there is love, you can either find a way or make one. We often see others through our own lens, but they usually don't have the same prescription. Find out what really makes the other person happy, and then do it.

Wine Grows Finer with Age under the Right Conditions

When a new restaurant opened near my workplace, it looked really nice, had great advertisements, and a friendly staff. The fact it was new and different from the usual place I ate lunch was really enticing, so I gradually stopped going to my usual lunch place because I was caught up with the new restaurant. My once favorite lunch restaurant now seemed old and was not as appealing.

Upon reflection, I was in a dilemma. Was the new place better, or was I just enjoying the next best thing? I then realized I was a victim of the latter. After some time had passed, I started craving the old restaurant.

This concept also occurs in our interpersonal relationships. If you don't watch out, you could lose something of great value that has been tried and tested for the next best thing. It now makes sense to me when I hear that a man left his wife of thirty years for someone he had known for less than six months. We think we will get a better deal from what is new and exciting, but the reality is it has not been proven like the old.

Giving up the real deal for a temporary hype could cost you in the long run. There are many attractions to going after the next best thing. Unfortunately, these attractions often only bring temporary satisfaction and excitement. When the hype goes down, you will be back to square one. So are you going to keep jumping ship? That becomes tiring after awhile. Luckily for me, it was only a restaurant, and the managers were happy to welcome my money and me back. But it is not always that simple in interpersonal relationships because the front door is not always left open.

A key to an enduring relationship is ensuring that it's developed within a suitable atmosphere. Wine only grows finer with age when stored at the right temperature. Under the wrong storage conditions, it ages twice as fast. Do you and your loved one continually choose to create an atmosphere that encourages and sustains growth? Are the choices you make daily leading you to the relationship of your dreams?

Remember, it all starts in the mind. Have a vision of where you want your relationship to be and decide to take daily action to help you get there. Make a list of the actions and changes you need to make on your road map to building a better relationship.

Faith versus Fear

The truth is, we all go through stuff in life, and how we handle these experiences can make us bitter or better. I have gone through many trying times that were stepping-stones to my becoming a better person. However, upon reflection, I realized that many of those experiences could have been more positive had I had a different perspective from my default pessimism.

The crucial thing about having problems is your perspective. Some say "half full or half empty" while others talk about the 80/20 principle. When a situation arises, you can view it either through the lens of fear or faith. The fear lens is like a magnifying lens: it makes the object look much larger and the fine details more obvious. But in reality, the object is not any larger, only your view is. Fear emphasizes the problem. Taking this approach leads to panic, and all objectivity flies out the window. The magnifying lens of fear has produced a mountain from a molehill.

The faith lens does the opposite, however, it focuses on the solution to the problem and emphasizes faith in God, thus making everything else seem insignificant. Imagine being in an airplane at thirty thousand feet. Everything appears small and inconsequential, doesn't it? This approach places your trust in God and not in your own strength to solve the problem. As a result, you have more peace and can go to bed at night knowing that God has your back.

Whenever a problem comes your way, remember to put on your faith lens.

Give People Room to Grow

I was reading the story of John's elementary school plant project. All the pupils in his biology class were given seeds to plant in empty milk cartons filled with soil. Each student planted his or her seed in the soil and then put the carton by the window. They watered their pots daily in anticipation that their seedlings would start to grow.

Some of the pupils started seeing signs of growth in their pots by day three of the project. John kept watering his pot, hoping and praying that, like the other pupils, he would see some growth in his pot. Days went bye, but John did not see any sign of growth. By the seventh day, John had lost all hope, so he decided to dig out his seed.

To his surprise, the seed looked different from when he planted it, so he showed it to his teacher. The teacher sighed and said it was not a different seed, but it was still growing. He said if only John had only waited one day longer, he would have seen the shoot of his seed. But it was a little too late; John had destroyed his harvest.

Looking back on my life, I see how impatient I have been when I have needed some things to change in the people closest to me. I unconsciously used myself as a yardstick in measuring their progress, which led to some burned bridges. A lesson I learned from John's experiment is that every person is unique, and it is important to give each one time to grow and discover who he or she is.

Throw Away the Exit Key

Marriage is like a package that comes in all shapes and sizes, and you can't know everything you are getting until you open it. Once opened, you will discover some things were not consistent with what you thought you knew about the product.

The gap between your expectations and actual experience can ruin a relationship. So before you open your package, have an open mind so you can enjoy its contents. There are no returns, refunds, or exchanges.

Receiving What You Cannot Give

Justin was three months away from his college graduation when he met Whitney through a mutual acquaintance, and their relationship grew serious. Justin knew he was moving away after graduation and that any relationship beyond platonic would not work for him, as he was not the type to commit to a long-distance relationship. But Justin felt like a million bucks around Whitney, so he could not resist the temptation to lead her on and chose not to communicate his fear of long-distance relationships because he was afraid of losing her. Whitney, however, wanted things to work and believed their love would help them through the distance.

Justin continued the relationship until he graduated and then moved on without Whitney. It was obvious that he was only interested in himself. He received Whitney's love, but when it was time to give it back through a long-distance relationship, he walked away.

Successful relationships thrive on the principle that everybody wins, which requires that both parties compromise. Justin refused to prevent his relationship with Whitney from getting intense. In the end, she was left with a broken heart. In relationships, when you receive and then choose to not give back, you may be shortchanging the other person.

Think about it.

Be Quick to Hear, Slow to Speak, and Slow to Anger

Many relationships have been ruined because of words spoken or actions taken at the spur of the moment. The Bible gives wise counsel on this issue in James 1:9, it reads, "Therefore, my beloved brethren, let every man be swift to hear, slow to speak, slow to anger."

According to Dr. Mike Murdock, "The kindest words are the ugliest words left unsaid." It is better to be silent and process the situation than to react spontaneously and be filled with regret. If needed, take a walk to cool off or change your environment.

Self-control always pays off.

What Happened to "Good Morning, America"?

What happened to "Good morning, America"? Am I the only one thinking about this? People don't say hello to each other anymore. Gone are the days when people wanted to say hello and really get to know who was sitting or living next to them. We seem to be more concerned about our little worlds and forget that our lives can be richer when we are connected with the people around us.

Technology has made the world a global village, and, as a result, we have become less dependent on personal interaction. This may be a great cost-saving measure for some businesses, but what is the impact on our communities? I can communicate through Facebook, Twitter, or Google-plus without getting personal, and I have noticed that people go straight to business when communicating at work. The common courtesy of "hello," "good morning," and "how are you?" has been thrown out the window. Even when you choose to be courteous, people really do not expect a response; before you respond, they are gone. No wonder billions of dollars are spent yearly on resolving office conflicts.

I believe we are wired to connect with each other, and technology should not replace personal contact. In my personal relationships, I too have fallen victim. Before the advent of Facebook, I would call loved ones on their birthdays to wish them well, but now I resort to social media to express my wishes.

Great relationships are not sustained on convenience; you have to make time to connect. Let's wake up. Technology should be used as a means to an end, not an end in itself.

Whatever You Take for Granted Becomes Grounded

I am sure everyone has heard the phrase, "You don't appreciate something until it is gone." I have decided this is not the motto I want to follow for my life. Thinking back, some situations would have been better handled if I had let some people know how much I valued them and their contribution to my life.

Whatever you appreciate increases in value, and whatever you neglect depreciates. The end result of depreciation is a loss of valuable connection and relationship. Hammerstein says it best: "A song is not a song until you sing it." Likewise, love is not love until you give it away. It is important that you realize the people in your life are not mind readers. It is not okay to only appreciate people in your mind; you need to let them know how much you care about them and not assume they know how you feel.

Assumptions kill relationships. Speak out, and show people you care.

Appreciate What You Have Before Its Too Late

If I showed the average person two identical paintings, one an original from Leonardo da Vinci and the other a cloned copy, chances are that someone may not be able to tell the difference, as it would require a trained and experienced eye to recognize the real thing from the fake. Likewise, not knowing the true worth of what or whom you have in your life can cost you a lot.

Similarly, have you ever looked for a missing item for hours just to find it in your pocket later? Frustrating, isn't it? Likewise, what you are looking for in a relationship may be so obvious that you miss seeing it in the people around you.

When I Meet the Right One …

Can one person be everything to you in a relationship? Can a single individual play the role of friend, parent, lover, mentor, doctor, confidant, gym partner, mind reader, and legal adviser? A dentist cannot help you with bone or joint problems. He would rather leave the final judgment to a specialist in that field.

Many of us are in a constant search for the "right" person, place, or thing and think when we get him, her, or it all will be well with us. However, the truth is, no one person or thing can meet all our needs and solve all our problems. That is far too heavy a load for any one person to carry. This expectation may have ruined many potential relationships because they did not fit our picture of "The One."

It is important that we let people care for us in the areas where they naturally excel and not where we expect their support. Having this mind-set will save us from this endless search and will open our hearts to let a variety of people be a blessing to us and be blessed by us, thus relieving the stress or burden on any one person.

There Is No Risk-Free Relationship

People are not perfect, and any time we connect or are in relationship with others, our imperfections will butt heads. Enter relationships looking for what you can give the other party and not what you can get from them. When both of you stop focusing on yourselves and start focusing on each other, the imperfections that seemed like a mountain will begin to disappear.

If you are looking for a risk-free relationship, you will need to exit the planet. Such relationships don't exist on Earth.

Are You a Nutrient or a Weed?

What do you have to offer? What do you bring to the table? Do you bring out the best in people? Do you bring relief, or are you that person who sucks the life out of a room? You may be gorgeous or generally likeable, but after a while, people will evaluate their relationship with you. They will ask themselves if they have become a better person by being around you.

In a vegetable garden, weeds compete and grow with the vegetables for the nutrients in the soil. If the weeds are not removed, they eventually affect the growth and quality of the vegetables. Likewise, if others see you as a weed in their lives, it is just a matter of time before they get rid of you.

People who act like weeds contribute nothing to relationships. They just keep taking, and as a result, they become a nuisance. If others see you as a nutrient, they want you in their lives because you make their world a better place. So look for ways you can be a nutrient to the people in your sphere of influence.

Relationships Are Not Ping-Pong

Table tennis, also known as Ping-Pong, is a fast-paced team sport that requires quick reactions. A skilled table tennis player is always two steps ahead of his opponent. A strategy for winning is to watch for his opponent's weak spots and capitalize on them. That strategy works well in table tennis but not in healthy relationships.

Healthy relationships are not based on fault-finding. Constantly pointing out your loved one's flaws is a quick way to lose him or her. Unlike table tennis, you cannot control your loved ones. Relationships are not competitions.

Those who try to control the people in their lives end up frustrated. It is not about you or the other party having his or her way but rather both of you working out a pattern where both of you win. Help your partner in the area of his or her weakness; complement one another. That is the true spirit of teamwork.

Good Counsel: Shade on a Sunny Day

On a hot sunny day, it is normal to seek a cooler place that provides temporary relief and safety from the blazing sun. Likewise, when life throws its worst at you don't isolate yourself. Seek relief in the shade of a trusted friend. I have gone through some trying times in my life, and what helped me was speaking with people who had gone through similar situations. Their counsel helped me get through my troubled times.

Love Is a Decision Only You Can Make

The foundation of friendship is love, but people often become disappointed because their mind-set is more contractual. In love, you don't always get back what you give or in the same measure you give. The saying that love is a decision and not mere feelings holds water.

Are You a Poison or a Catalyst?

According to the Merriam-Webster's dictionary, a poison is a substance that kills, injures, or impairs while a catalyst is an agent that provokes or speeds significant change or action[3]. Do you know that your words can kill, injure, and discourage or can encourage positive change and action in others? So, are you a catalyst or a poison?

Since our words can have an impact on others, it is important that we have control over our lips. I have observed that most people tend to remember the negative words spoken rather than the positive ones. I remember in high school when I had the highest score in my first advanced math homework assignment, the teacher announced to the whole class that he was surprised I had the highest score. That experience crushed my confidence because I focused more on what the teacher thought of me rather than on my abilities. I eventually dropped the class because I allowed my teacher's evaluation of me define the quality of my work.

Similarly, I heard an interesting story when my friend, Gaby, told me she never allowed anyone to take her pictures. On inquiry, she said that when she was little, her friends and siblings teased her about her smile and her looks. That memory had stuck with her, and although she was gorgeous, Gaby did not feel pretty enough for the camera.

Another friend of mine told me a story about a friend who had difficulty hearing, but he was able to speak well. One day, his sister teased him that it was awkward he could speak but could not hear what anyone was saying. He took his sister's words to heart and has never spoken in public since that day. She meant it as a joke, but her words were a poison to him. A similar example occurred when a thoughtless reporter called Karen Carpenter

"Richard's chubby sister." As a result, Karen developed anorexia nervosa and died at the young age of thirty-three.

Some parents have ridiculed or spoken over their children in anger, and their harsh words eventually came true. The solution is not to keep silent because even that can be misinterpreted. We need to learn to speak positive, affirming words to others. There is certainly room for correction, but we need to speak the truth in love and not in anger. Speaking while we are hurt will only hurt others.

We have no control over people's words, but we do have control over what we hear and how we interpret it. It is important that we become selective hearers. If we keep listening to negative reports, we will eventually get discouraged. We need to reassess the people we give permission to speak into our lives. It may be necessary to love some people from a distance so their negativity doesn't rub off on us.

Finally, you may want to think about what you are thinking about. You can control your response when others speak to you, but how do you protect yourself from your negative, destructive thoughts? Your mind does not exist in a vacuum, so you have to fill it with positivity. When I find myself thinking negative thoughts, I audibly reject them and make faith-based confessions instead. Remember the words of Mahatma Gandhi:

> Watch your thoughts, they become words.
> Watch your words, they become actions.
> Watch your actions, they become habits.
> Watch your habits, they become your character.
> Watch your character, it becomes your destiny.

You become your thoughts and the conclusions you draw from them. No one keeps a poison for keepsake, but everyone desires a catalyst. If you want to make a positive difference in people's lives, follow the words of Abraham Lincoln, "A drop of honey catches more flies than a gallon of gall."

Tired of Being Lonely? Find, Attract, and Keep

Find: Imagine for a minute you want to sell a great idea or product that you know will make a big difference in your community. There are some things I am guessing you would do or consider.

After creating good content and packaging for your product, you would start telling your family, friends, colleagues, and everyone in your circle about your product. The next step would be to make the product available online through Facebook, Twitter, and MySpace. You could follow this up by advertising through Google, Amazon, and local retailers, such as Walmart and Target. All the networking and advertising for your product would be aimed toward increasing the success for your product. So, friend, in order to climb your social network and connect with others, you will increase your chances of meeting people by going where the people are.

Attract and keep: Great packaging will increase interest in your product. The packaging is your personality and character, which must always be under construction. The real question here is, would people find you (your product) as what you have been advertising? The answer would determine the authenticity of your product and your credibility. If your clients like what they see, they will stay with you. If they get more than what they expect, they will tell their friends. If you are consistent delivering what you have advertised, people will keep coming back. That's the secret of establishing yourself as the real deal.

Check Your Guest List

Athletes are particularly aware that the type of clothing they wear can make a big difference in their performance. Imagine a 100-meter sprinter wearing boots and jeans or a marathon runner wearing a space suit. We have all worn jeans and boots at some point in our lives, but wearing them for a race would be heavy baggage for the athlete and would hinder the performance of even the best sprinters.

In our lives, we all have passengers we are carrying in the sea of our hearts. Some are a delight while others can sink our ship. I believe it is important that we cultivate the habit of checking our guest list to ensure that none of our guests is toxic or constitutes a burden that sinks our ship. The times I matured in my life was when I was connected to positive, encouraging individuals. The lowest points of my life were when I was connected with the wrong people.

It is important you know yourself and where you are going before you start admitting people onto the deck of your life. Can you imagine going to the airport and telling the clerk at the counter that you want a ticket to anywhere? Many people have had countless disappointments because they had no clue as to who they were and what they wanted in a relationship. This often leads to people becoming protégés of themselves, resulting in frustration in both parties. In order to develop meaningful relationships, it is important to know your own values and beliefs.

Bottom line, be careful about those you allow to influence you, as they can make or mar you. It is true that in the ship of our lives, there are some people we do not have a choice but to have on our decks, such as a spouse, children, coworkers, boss, etc. However, you do have a choice as to how much influence and impact they have on you. Some of your passengers may be carrying excess luggage, so you will need to say good-bye so your ship does not sink. Other relationships may need to be redefined with new boundaries drawn.

So, friend, what are you all about? Do you enjoy your own company? You need to celebrate your strengths and be at peace with your weaknesses. When you do, you will become irresistible.

Plant Your Seed

I remember my excitement when I planted my first vegetable garden. I cleared the plot, removed any weeds, and tilled the soil. The next steps were to plant my seeds, water them, and hope they would blossom.

Likewise, as an individual, you need to plant your idea and run with it. A seed is useless if it is not planted. You may have thousands of ideas, but it is important you give your intention your full attention. Not all your plans will be successful the first time around, but the best gift you can give yourself is to try them out.

Tyler Perry, an American actor, director, screenwriter, playwright, producer, author, and songwriter was named Forbes' highest paid man in entertainment, earning about $130 million dollars between May 2010 and May 2011. Tyler said the secret of his success was his believing in his dream and focusing solely on it. He had produced so many plays that were unsuccessful, but each of his failed attempts served as training for him to become better. Tyler Perry is known worldwide today because he planted his idea and nurtured it.

Success gives birth to success. If you can get one idea to work, it will lead to the success of others. A well-watered plant will give rise to other plants. The most successful companies are known mainly for one product.

Focus on your dream, and keep at it. Believe in your dream, and it will surely come to pass.

Think of God as Your GPS

Do you remember when you had an important meeting in the middle of nowhere and you had to depend on your GPS to get you there? Some parts of the route seemed familiar while the remainder of the journey was filled with uncertainty. You really wanted to trust the GPS at such a crucial time, but doubts and what-ifs kept clouding your reasoning. However, since it was all you had, you had to trust it to get you there safely. Remember when you missed a couple of turns and got mad at yourself? Suddenly, you heard the GPS say, "Rerouting," and soon you were back on track. After a journey like an emotional roller coaster, you finally got to your destination.

Likewise, God can be your life's GPS, and you will have to trust him to get you where you need to be on time and safely. It is easier to trust when you are taking a familiar route, but God will take you on an unfamiliar route to your destination.

No matter how many times you miss your exit, God always reroutes you. It may take longer, but you will eventually reach your final destination. Trust him, relax, and enjoy the ride.

Failure and Success in Life

Lessons from a Failed Experiment

I am a scientist, so I know the road leading to discovery is not a smooth one. I have performed many experiments that ended with unpredictable results. This was often frustrating because of the time and resources I had invested in the experiments.

I grew tired of my emotions swinging like a pendulum when I performed these experiments, so I decided to change my perspective. I realized that the unsuccessful experiments were actually providing useful information that would help me reach the right end result. Anytime I had an experiment that did not go according to plan, I tried to find out what went wrong and noted it for future experiments.

Likewise, in our lives, there is no such thing as being a failure. We only become one if we choose to remain a victim of our circumstances. Life does not always go the way we intend, but for every detour in life, there is always a lesson to be learned or an opportunity to be grasped. The popular soda drink Coca-Cola was discovered when pharmacist John Pemberton attempted to create a cure for headaches.

Even unexpected outcomes can be a blessing in disguise. Penicillin, the first and now one of the most widely used antibiotics in the world, was created in 1928 when Sir Alexander Fleming didn't clean up his workstation before leaving for vacation. When he returned, he noticed there was a strange fungus on some of his cultures. To his surprise, he discovered that bacteria didn't seem to thrive near those cultures. In 1945, Fleming later won the Nobel Prize in Physiology or Medicine alongside Sir Howard Florey and Ernst Boris Chain

It can be frustrating when things do not go our way, especially when we have done our part. When that happens, we must take a step back and ask ourselves, "What can I learn from this?" Remember that some of the greatest discoveries that made history and changed lives occurred by chance. There is no such thing as a failed experiment if a lesson has been learned.

Better Sorry Than Safe

A rubber band is only useful when it is stretched. The rubber band has two states, relaxed and stretched. The relaxed state of a rubber band is not useful for anything, but the stretched state is where its purpose is maximized. Likewise, people who want to achieve great things cannot afford to remain in their relaxed state, or comfort zone.

High flyers in all walks of life have an all-or-nothing attitude. Think of any great work of art. It took many, many hours to create the masterpiece. Humans did not land on the moon out of convenience. It was a vision that was conceived and birthed through hard work and determination. The Wright brothers, who invented the world's first successful airplane, encountered many failed attempts. It was not an easy task, but difficult did not mean impossible for the duo.

You cannot play it safe and expect to make an impact at the same time. Playing it safe is living in a relaxed state, which is below your potential—filled with regrets (woulda-coulda-shoulda) is not a happy place to be. It is always better to aim high. Even if you miss your target, your end result is still good.

Put First Things First

As I was growing up, my father always traveled around the world. The toys and gifts from different continents were great, but as I grew older, the gifts didn't mean as much anymore. I wanted my father to attend my sport activities or watch me perform in the choir. The presents were great, but they were never a substitute for my dad's presence. If I had had a choice, I would have chosen his presence over the presents.

Similarly, in your relationships with loved ones, your presence is the cake while your presents are the icing on the cake. I am sure you would agree that eating only icing is not the best health decision.

Many times we have good intentions, but we need to step it up a notch and do something about them. You may have a crazy work schedule, but this is about quality time, not quantity time. What is quality time? It is the intentional time you spend with your loved ones that fill them up until the next time.

We all make time for what we consider important. So the question is, Do you give quality time to the people or things that matter most to you? For me, it is faith, family, and career. What are your priorities?

When a young man falls to the ground, he looks forward, but when an old man falls down he looks backwards.—Nigerian Proverb

I saw my eleven-month-old son fall down while taking his first steps. He got back up only to fall again, not realizing that his shoelace was the culprit.

When we fall down in life, do we just get back up and do exactly what we did before, or, like the wise old men, do we take a step back, evaluate the situation, and see why we fell? When we do this, we are better able to make an informed decision because this prevents us from falling into the same situation again.

Step back and see what is causing the problem.

Work Friendships Are Important

The office is for work, and it is important to always keep that in mind. Let your productivity and accomplishments speak for you rather than try to be a buddy to your supervisors to climb the ranks. No one can put an embargo or cap on where love or friendships find you, but there are some lines that can be crossed in work friendships that could have a serious impact on your career.

Your personal friends don't consider your mistakes as permanent damage, but your workmates could label them as incompetence, so be sure you know the difference between a colleague and a friend at work before disclosing personal information. Tom Rath, leader of Gallup's research and leadership consulting worldwide, in his book *Vital Friends* showed that cultivating true friendships at work increased the productivity of workers, contrary to popular belief.

Let's be honest. All of us have either felt better going to work because of a friend or worse because of a particular colleague. I have experienced both, and I prefer the former. So you may want to consider deepening the relationships you have at work because a happy you at work transfers to other areas of your life. In building work friendships like any other meaningful relationships, remember to maintain a healthy distance so as to not burn each other out.

Risk-Takers Are Dream Makers

Have you ever wondered, "What if Christopher Columbus never took that trip?" If he hadn't, the story of America would be different. What if Bill Gates or Steve Jobs thought that their ideas were not worth pursuing? After all, they were college dropouts. Helen Keller could have let her physical challenges and limitations be an excuse to live a mediocre life, or Oprah Winfrey could have thought that no woman could have her own show.

Risk is what separates the great from the average. We all have had "What if it doesn't work?" running in our heads, as we all fear failing or of being rejected. Christopher Columbus, Bill Gates and Steve Jobs are all regarded as American Greats today because they faced their fears and took risks. In business, the greater the risk, the greater the opportunity for a huge return. Taking no risk means gaining no significant return. What risks are you prepared to take regarding your future?

Leaders Are Born and Made

There is an ongoing debate as to whether leaders are made or born. I believe it is both.

Some people believe that leadership like any other skill can be learned. While there is some truth to this, but to assume that leadership is mutually exclusive of talent, acquired skills, and knowledge is like saying you can learn to sing like Mariah Carey or paint like Leonardo da Vinci if you attend the right school. Skills and knowledge without talent can take you only so far; at best, you become a good leader but not a great leader. I believe in order to become a great leader, you must possess some innate qualities.

Imagine someone with tremendous sales talent. In order for him to maintain high productivity, he must believe in what he is selling and have a good knowledge of the product. These two factors coupled with his natural talent for persuasion are what make him successful. But remove one of the factors, and you will see a negative impact on his performance.

If you train someone in the art of selling a product and try to infuse some passion into him without him having natural sales talent, he will probably be a mediocre salesperson as opposed to someone who has all three factors. Likewise, you can teach people leadership skills, but if they do not have passion for leading others, they will fail in comparison to someone who does.

What Is Fueling You?

Cadillacs and Ferraris are known as luxury automobiles, but all the attributes that make them special become useless on an empty gas tank. At this point, they cannot perform their basic functions. However, you will enjoy their benefits when they become fueled.

Similarly, we all have potential, but this is similar to having a car without any gas. Potential is good, but it has no benefit if it does not contribute to the community, others, or ourselves. Action fuels our intentions and produces results while fear stifles us and makes us victims, which produces failure.

It is easier to take action when you are passionate about something. Make a list of the things you are passionate about, and match them with your talents. This combination will surely ignite something in you. Whatever fuels you (action or fear) will ultimately determine if you succeed or fail.

Delete, Install, and Update

I remember a time at the airport when a frowning customer service agent said, "Your luggage is three pounds overweight." She gave me the option of reducing the weight of my baggage or paying the fines. Neither option was pleasant, but in order to get on the flight, I had to choose one. Likewise, in life we sometimes carry excess baggage from past relationships and experiences, and this can hinder us from getting to the people we want to be with or the places we want to go. If we don't get rid of the excess baggage, it will cost us.

I had difficulty opening a file on my computer, and I found out the reason was I did not have Adobe software installed. Luckily for me, the software was free and my problem was easily solved. I learned from that experience that what I do not know could cost me. Ignorance is never an excuse, so I made up my mind to broaden my horizons by learning a little about a lot of things.

It is important to be open to paradigm shifts, as it is the way to learn something new and to improve ourselves. There is more than one way to do what we are doing, so we must find those other ways and learn them. It could save us time, money, and even our jobs.

I get regular messages from my computer telling me to update my programs if they are to function properly. There have been times when I have ignored the messages and have paid the price of having a slow, dysfunctional computer. In like manner, we need to stay updated with the people in our lives and current with new technology in our careers so we don't become outdated.

Life Is Not Mathematics

I have a five-year goal for myself. I also have weekly and daily goals. My planning has really helped me in achieving many goals, but I have discovered that even with the best of plans, some things might alter the original one. So it is wise to factor in a bit of uncertainty when planning your life and career so that when things do happen, you are in a better frame of mind to handle them objectively.

Disability Is Not Lack of Ability

Some people are born with physical challenges while others became physically challenged as a result of an illness or injury. Many have internal disabilities resulting from experiences, such as abuse, a broken home, or a bitter relationship experience. It is unfortunate that some of us allow the disability in one area of their lives to define the rest of it.

Hello, friend, disability is not a lack of ability. If you can envision it, you can achieve it. Andrea Bocelli, who became blind at age twelve after a football accident, is a great musician today and is the best-selling solo artist in the history of classical music. Andrea refused to spend the rest of his life living on a disability check. He is now widely regarded as the most popular Italian and classical singer in the world.

Gloria Allred was raped at gunpoint while she was on vacation in Mexico. From this devastating experience, Gloria went from being a victim to a survivor to finally a fighter for women's rights. Today she is known as one of the foremost human rights lawyers in America. Her traumatic experience was a defining moment for her, and she now channels all her energy into speaking for women in despair. Gloria refused to allow her past to incapacitate her future.

Where there is a will there is a way. You can move beyond your disabilities. To start the journey, you need to have a mental picture of where you want to be. You can excel regardless of what has happened in the past. The only thing you cannot do is what you have not yet tried to do.

If you want to walk fast, walk alone. If you want to walk far, walk together.—African Proverb

Everyone says life can be likened to a marathon and not a sprint. If you want to run a marathon, it is great to have company, as you will need the encouragement, care, and support for the distance. I remember when I started running I needed some motivation, so I started running with a group of people. The first group always left me behind because it was obvious I was dead weight on their team while another group was very patient with me and gave me room to come up to speed with them over a period of three months. I chose to stay with the team that helped me be a better me, and their investment in me paid off. After some months, I was able to inspire the group to run longer distances and to vary our workout plan, which benefited the group. Some of my friends in the former group run marathons regularly, which requires a lot of teamwork regarding motivation and preparation for the sport. The same goes for mountain climbing; you need a good team when navigating dangerous terrain. Sprint runners depend solely on themselves and so can go only far as their energy allows. If you have a big dream, idea, or goal you want to accomplish, you are going to need a team to make your dream a reality. A true team player holds his side of the bargain and does not wait for others to make things happen for him. If you can accomplish your dream by yourself, your dream is not big enough, as none of us is better alone than all of us together.

No Condition Is Permanent

One thing you should remember is that no condition is permanent. The only constant thing is change itself. Do not underestimate yourself. Just because you come from a dysfunctional background does not mean your future is going to end up the same way.

The servant today can be a leader tomorrow, so be careful how you treat people. I remember the story about a former slave, Elizabeth Keckley, who had a dream of gaining her freedom and designing clothes for the nobility of society. She eventually gained her freedom through her excellence in designing clothes and supported her former slave owners through her business when their business was failing. Elizabeth made clothes for the rich and famous, and her designs even caught the attention of the First Lady of the United States, Mary Todd Lincoln, and Elizabeth eventually became her seamstress and confidant and was the first person Mrs. Lincoln called when her husband was assassinated. Keckley, though a former slave, became an entrepreneur.

This principle also occurs in the reverse. If you are great at what you do, you must keep reinventing yourself because there are others waiting to take your place. From history, we know that England, Rome, Egypt, and Germany once led the world, but it is America today. The United States must keep coming up with innovative technology and purposeful leadership if it does not want to join the ranks of other countries in the history books.

The citizens of Egypt and Liberia had suffered under their dictators, but now they are free. Your voice, justice, rights, and freedom may be delayed for a while, but no one can take away your dreams. So keep dreaming of a better tomorrow because no condition is permanent.

A Solution-Oriented Personality (SOP) or a Problem-Oriented Personality (POP)?

Do you have an SOP or a POP? It is possible to switch between the two modes depending on the situation. Solution-oriented personalities see themselves as a solution to problems rather than part of the problem and take responsibility for the world around them. They are not people-fixers and are more geared toward making decisions and taking action that solves conflicts rather than kicking them down the road. Their actions may involve confronting a situation or letting sleeping dogs lie.

Problem-oriented personalities, on the other hand, are not trouble-promoters, but they make decisions and take actions that create an artificial peace in the short term. In the long term, their actions or inactions actually worsen or escalate conflicts or situations in their lives or the world around them. They are people who ignore the elephant in the room, so the situation continues to deteriorate.

Solution-oriented people are flexible and will play whatever roles will ensure their team's success. As Steven Covey illustrates in his book, "The 7 Habits of Highly Effective People", it is about having a win-win mentality. The lyrics "You were my strength when I was weak, you were my voice when I couldn't speak, you were my eyes when I couldn't see, you saw the best there was in me [4]" sang by Celine Dion are a good example as to how we can be distinct to people at different periods in their lives.

Only One Key to Unlock a Set Of Doors

I had about twenty keys on my keychain, and I tried at least four or five of them to find the right one for my office. This constantly frustrated me, and I feared breaking a key in the lock. Likewise, in our relationships, I don't believe we have to experience several broken hearts before we finally find the right person.

You discover who you are by making friends and connecting with people and eventually learn what works for you. It is okay to make mistakes before becoming exclusive with one person because that is how you learn. You could cause a lot of damage if you see your relationship as a practice test and your partner sees it as an exam.

The problem with serial dating is you could be worse off than you started because you could be using a past relationship lens to filter potential ones. Lee Segall said, "A man with two watches is never quite sure of the time.[5]" When you go shopping and find a bargain, I hope you seize the opportunity and not wonder if another store has a similar or better discount. You could, but once that bargain is gone, it is gone for good. You may have just lost a golden opportunity.

I believe many people have been in good relationships, but because they wanted to explore or find out if there was something better, they left a great relationship for a good one. Think about it, the current statistics of divorce in America is alarming. This shows there is something amiss with the current dating system. No one wants to take the same exam a dozen times before passing. I believe that should hold true for relationships as well. What you need is adequate preparation so when the right person comes along, you are ready. It is better to get it right than try to make it right.

Life Exams Are Not Dated

Like most of us, we often receive some advance notice of important deadlines, which often gives us time to prepare. There were some exams I took in college that were impromptu, and I wished I had been better prepared for them.

I woke up one morning and walked downstairs to begin my daily routine. Everything seemed normal until I discovered that many things where out of place. Finally, it dawned on me that my house had been burgled. I was frightened and angry yet happy at the same time. I was thankful I had not been hurt, but I did not receive any warning from the burglars that my valuables would be stolen.

My aunt didn't have any warning when her house was hit by a tornado. While there are many things in life we can prepare for, such as having insurance in case of an accident, flood, or theft, in reality, the exams of life are not dated. How you respond during those moments depend on how well you have prepared. Can you imagine a firefighter responding to a fire without any training? So start preparing now; the exams of life are not dated.

Results Today, Action Tomorrow

This is the classic slogan for procrastinators. They desire results, but they delay the actions that will produce the changes in their lives. No wonder nothing happens despite their strong desires.

Nothing works until you work at it. Let's borrow a little inspiration from termites. They do a little at a time to accomplish a great task. Success cannot be attained by a fire brigade approach. You need to be consistent, which is where the power to produce results lies. I am a very busy person, but in order to write this book, I decided to work on it for twenty minutes every day for two years.

You may never accomplish every item on your to-do list, but you can cross each one off, one day at a time.

What You Know Is Not What Is Important

Smokers know that smoking is dangerous to their health. People who have any form of addiction know that giving into their cravings could harm them. Many of us know that exercise is good for our health, and although we make resolutions year after year, we return to the same habits. So it is not what we know that is important, but what we do with what we know.

Mark Twain says it best, "A person who does not read has no advantage over someone who cannot read." Knowing and doing what you know separates you from the crowd. Knowledge is only powerful when it is applied.

A Work In Progress

It is important to always wear this badge as a reminder that life is a journey and not a destination. There is no present without a past. Yeah, we have all made some mistakes, taken some wrong turns, and wished we could turn back the hands of time. That is the past, so get over it. Whatever your situation or circumstances, as long as you have air in your lungs and courage in your heart, you can have a comeback. Everyone thought that General Motors had reached the end of the road, but it has shown, in the words of Helen Keller, "The bend of a road is not the end of a road."

We live in a warp-speed era. We want everything in an instant. We want faster Internet, computers, cars, etc. Unfortunately, we are not able to keep up with this speed in our interpersonal relationships. Many infomercials that focus on weight loss often show the before-and-after photos of a person, but they do not show the process. They do not show all the hard work, near dropouts, sleepless nights, tears, pain, and fears, thus creating unrealistic expectations.

The truth is, it takes time to build a solid relationship, to lose weight, and to build a better you. The road to success is always under construction and is not easy. It requires breaking things down and building new ones. It is a messy process, but the final outcome makes it all worthwhile. Anyone who really wants to be physically fit knows it is not a one-time commitment. It is a lifestyle. You must make decisions on a daily basis to support your resolution.

Friend, if you take a bold step each day toward your goal, you will reach your final destination. The road will not always be smooth, but keep a picture of your end goal in mind. This will give you some motivation during the down times.

Dynamic Success Combo—Pray, Pay, and Play

Praying is acknowledging that you cannot do something by yourself, so you invite divine assistance. Paying your dues after praying is crucial, as both are not mutually exclusive. You are actually adding flesh to the skeleton by creating an opportunity for your prayers to be answered.

Playing after praying and paying is the last piece of the puzzle. You have given your best, let God do the rest, and relax and enjoy the great things ahead.

Your Gift Will Make a Way for You

Are you naturally good at what you do? Do you like what you do? Do you like what you do and think you are good at it, or are you ignorant of your gifts? Are you living your dream or someone else's? Your answer to these questions will help you prioritize your efforts based on your natural gifts and talents.

The Council for Exceptional Children (CEC) defines giftedness as "That precious endowment of potentially outstanding abilities that allows a person to interact with the environment with remarkably high levels of achievement and creativity[6]." According to Merrian-Webster's dictionary, *grace* is defined as charming or attractive traits or characteristics[7]. These characteristics enable you to function at your highest potential. Albert Einstein said, "Everybody is a genius. But if you judge a fish by its ability to climb a tree, it will live its whole life believing that it is stupid." If this statement has any validity, which I believe it does, it means that if we are able to discover and have faith in our gifts, we can excel in whatever we do.

The question is, How do we discover our gifts? From the CEC definition, our gifts indicate those areas we have high levels of achievement and creativity. Whitney Houston was a great singer. Her talent could not be taught in any school. We either have it or we don't. Our creativity will be sparked in the areas of our talents, and we will find fulfillment in the area of our gifting. We will excel in areas where others struggle when we operate in our gifting.

Natural ability is never an excuse to be mediocre. We must develop and cultivate our talents because they get better with use. A person with much experience can excel over a person who is gifted but lazy. Malcolm

Gladwell makes an excellent illustration of this point in his book *Outliers* where he writes that people who have excelled in their field had to invest a minimum of ten thousand hours regardless of their gifting level.

Imagine those who naturally excel in problem solving, science, singing, athletics, acting, building things, poetry, etc. I would expect these individuals are attending or planning to attend institutions that will help them develop their talents. But in reality, many gifted people do not invest in their gifts due to ignorance, fear, economics, or complacency. Other reasons include family pressure or dissuasion in pursuing their dreams.

Can you imagine how a fish out of water would feel? It would be exhausted and frustrated because it is not functioning in the area of its design. A mentor of mine once told me that if he could do things over again, he would become a lawyer. He said that when he sees a lawyer, something within tells him that is what he was meant to be. I was shocked because he was very successful in his career in finance. So is it possible to be successful when you don't operate in your gifts? Absolutely. The real question should be, are you fulfilled? Fulfillment, or lack of it, is a good indicator as to whether you are operating in your gifting or not.

So what are you going to do? Are you going to take the easy way out and play it safe? I like the words of Henry Ford, "Those who never make mistakes work for those who do." Not investing in your gifts can be likened to living like a fish out of water. There is a place for everyone who dares to live his or her dreams.

Focusing on your gifts does not guarantee you will never fail, but if you keep at it, your gifts will one day announce you to the world and will make your dreams come alive. Do not settle for less, you are more than second best. There is no one else like you. What you love is what you will be best at, so invest in it. Stop trying to fix your weaknesses but rather focus on building your strengths. It is time to make your passion your profession; your gift will make a way for you.

Today: The Future You Prepared for Yesterday

Early preparation prevents poor performance. Not having a plan for your life is a plan to fail. Nothing great happens by chance. Success is not an accident; it requires hard work, strategizing, and making the most of opportunities. In today's economy, you need more than hard work to succeed. You must have your goals and dreams ingrained in your mind. The vision of your future will sustain you during the tough times.

Whatever you are experiencing now is the result of how you invested yesterday. So to have a better future, it is vital to use today wisely. Mike Murdock said that champions are not made in the ring but recognized in one. A medal is actually an acknowledgment of the preparation. Exams of life are always a good reward for the well prepared.

You may be ill prepared in some areas of your life and are paying the price right now. That's okay, we all have made our fair share of mistakes. But what are you going to do now? Having a pity party, blaming others, or avoiding the issues will only bring temporary relief.

You need to pick up where you left off and jump back into the ring of life. Your past experiences should have equipped you for where you are now. Whatever does not break you makes you stronger and wiser. Quitting should never be a word in your dictionary. You have what it takes, so why not start again by taking that first step?

Your Background Does Not Put Your Back on the Ground

People are generally interested in results rather than excuses. Lazy and incompetent people make excuses to remain victims while achievers use the same excuses as springboards to attain their goals.

You may have had a challenging past, but you can channel all that emotion and energy toward your success story. Think about it. Just like a hard ground provides bounce for a tennis ball, your difficult background can help catapult you to the next level. Your background is meant to serve as a stepping-stone to higher ground. You just have to decide which team you are on, Team Victor or Team Victim. Just because your parents were alcoholics does not mean you are going to be one. There is no doubt that some backgrounds predispose people to certain tendencies more than others, but you can fight it and win the battle.

My friend Tom had a troubled, impoverished childhood. He was abandoned as a kid and moved from one foster home to the other. This motivated him to be one of the best students in college, and he graduated with a 3.9 GPA. Tom's negative experiences drove him toward excellence. On the other hand, some of his siblings played the blame game and remained victims. Tom is very successful today and helps his siblings whenever he can.

At eighteen, Dawn Loggins was abandoned and homeless. She worked as a janitor between her studies to make ends meet. She even requested candles from a staff member at Burns High School so she could do her homework at night. Despite the odds, Dawn was the best student in her class and was admitted to five colleges, including Harvard.

Lebron James came from a dysfunctional neighborhood and was the son of a convict, yet he didn't let that limit him. He was determined and focused. Today, he is celebrated all over the world.

Your setback can set the stage for your comeback. What will you choose to overcome?

Fill In the Blanks

I recall tests that required filling in the blanks with the most appropriate phrase from a given list of options. It was often exciting when I chose the correct option because it made the sentence come alive. Something we can learn from the fill-in-the-blank method is to give people what they want and not what we think they need. Relationships suffer setbacks when people are on different pages.

When looking for a job, we often tailor our resume to the job description. When relating with our boss or manager at work, we often find out his or her interests and then use those topics to engage or connect with him or her. When I want to connect with children, I usually find out from their parents what really interests them. In a similar way, when connecting with people, find out what makes them tick and be that to them. Success is meeting people at the place of their needs.

To be successful with people, find their need and meet it. An easy way to do that is to ask them.

Vision Does Not Come from Watching Television

After a long day, it is easy to relax in front of the TV, watching your favorite shows. But an excess of this activity is mind numbing. How many hours do you spend in front of the TV each day? Are those hours spent or invested? Think about it. Have those shows really added value to your life in the long term? David Dunstan of Monash University in Melbourne conducted a study that showed that Aussies who watched four or more hours of TV a day were 46 percent more likely to die during a six-and-a-half-year period than those who watched less than two hours a day. This conclusion did not surprise Dr. Gerald Fletcher, a cardiologist and spokesman for the American Heart Association, because sedentary living encourages heart disease. Also, an extended time watching television encourages overeating, which can lead to obesity. Pediatricians report that too much time spent watching TV is not good for children, as it can affect their brain and behavioral development. Many parents now know the importance of reducing TV time and its correlation with their children's grades.

Your life is more than being a spectator or cheering for others from the sidelines. Your vision could create TV shows, but you cannot make that happen if you are always glued to your plasma screen. You can choose to develop healthy habits. Take a walk, play sports, or reconnect with a friend. I realized the amount of time I was spending on social media websites was not adding long-term value to my life, so I decided to reduce that time significantly, which ultimately gave birth to this book.

Okay Is Boring

Many of us are content living the "okay life," which is settling for mediocrity and accepting what life throws at us. Imagine what the world would have missed if prolific author and activist Helen Keller had not made an effort to overcome her fears of the world. Unable to see or hear, Helen had every excuse to not accomplish anything in her life, but she refused to receive handouts and be mediocre. Instead, she chose to give life her best shot regardless of her circumstances and became the first deaf and blind person to earn a bachelor's degree. She then became an advocate for people with disabilities and an internationally renowned lecturer. An inspiration to people all over the world, Helen Keller has shown all of us that the only limitations we have are the ones we allow.

So what has been holding you back from reaching for the stars? A journey of a thousand miles begins with a single step. The road may be long, but with perseverance, you can reach your destination. If you are going to do something significant, why not start now? When there is a will, there is a way. Just do it.

Excuse or Be Excused: Either Way, You Lose

Are you tired of making excuses or being excused for personal actions or inaction? There is always something or someone else to blame besides you. I remember taking a taxi to the airport one time and asking the driver if he could drive more carefully. He responded, "It is not my fault. The road is bad." Sure, the road could have been better, but he could have avoided the potholes and driven a bit slower. But instead, he blamed the road for his bad driving.

If excuses are your way out of situations, the end result is often your friends, loved ones, or employers taking the exit door. There are a few things in life you want to keep to yourself, and excuses are one of them. When you point a finger at someone else, the remaining four are pointing back at you. My friend, check yourself before you wreck yourself.

Chase Your Dreams

When you really want something, you go after it. Remember that dream job or date you had? I am guessing you did not consult a committee to validate your desire. You pursued it because it was something of value to you.

Talk is cheap. Anyone can talk, but few follow through. What are you doing about those ideas you have on your mind? Facebook, Yahoo, and Disney were once only ideas. The difference is that the founders of these great organizations actually woke up from their dreams and lived them.

Chase your dreams; it is the proof of your desire. When I campaigned to be president of the Students Chemical Society of Nigeria while in college not many people thought I was capable of the job. But I knew I could move the organization a step higher. It was a well-contested election, but I emerged the winner with a comfortable margin. My team and I were able to make significant contributions, which was widely acknowledged with awards.

If you want something, go for it. Stop talking, and start taking action.

Whatever You Build Will Last

It amuses me how people want to have great relationships "just like that" without paying the price of hard work (quality time, listening, patience, etc.). It takes time for the pebbles on the beach to become smooth. It's been a work in progress all the time.

Even if you and the other person "click," it will not automatically stay that way. For any relationship worth having, there is a price to pay. Stop shopping for ready-made, convenient relationships. Open your tool kit today, and start digging. Whatever you build will last.

What You Love to Give Never Runs Out

Whatever you love to give never runs out. Seems ironic, doesn't it? Take stock of what you love to give and see if you have ever run out of it. Perhaps it's giving a smile, making people happy, or money. Whatever it is, you will find you have a lot of it and even some in reserve. The reason it never runs dry is because of the law of reciprocity, which says that whatever you do will come back to you. If you like helping people, you will find people want to help you in return.

The law of reciprocity works indirectly. For example, you may refer your friend for a job and then someone else informs you of a great opportunity. But it is crucial that you do not expect something in return from the people you help.

Why not take the reciprocity challenge? You can start by looking for ways to meet other people's needs. This may be directly or referring them to someone else who can help. Whatever you make happen for others, God will make happen for you.

You Are an Original

I needed to verify some documents recently, so I visited a justice of the peace. At the office, they asked to see the originals because photocopies were not accepted. I tried to prevail upon the clerk to accept my photocopies, as they were true copies, but she said that some clients had altered copied documents in the past.

Likewise, people want to be in a relationship with the real you, not who you wish you were. You are the real deal. It is time to start living and not get submerged in the shadows of the past. You are a voice, not an echo. You are an answer to someone's prayer. You are not perfect; no one is. But you have what it takes. You are a winner, not a quitter. You are not part of the problem but part of the solution.

Some people need what you have. Discover them. Celebrate your originality.

If You Are Not Going to Eat It, Don't Go Near It

I love donuts. I wanted to shed a few pounds, but my love for donuts was definitely not going to help me accomplish my goal, so I decided to take a break from my favorite pastry. I changed my route to work in the mornings because there was a donut shop on that path, and this helped me reduce my cravings. After all, out of sight is out of mind.

I take my old route now, but the abstinence from donuts was needed to help me build inner strength and motivation. I achieved results from eating healthy and cutting down on pastries, so I was not about to go back. Now I eat a donut once a week, and it is much easier for me to say no when I am tempted.

If you are not planning on eating an item, don't go near it. This principle is so crucial to living a healthy lifestyle. Know your limitations or temptations, and stay far away from them. You may need to change your route or put structures in place to guard you from whatever lures you away from your goal. Many great people have fallen because they convinced themselves they could handle a situation, but they eventually got sucked into it. This is where the wisdom to run wins over the strength to fight.

The Scars of Yesterday Have No Power Over The Joys of Tomorrow

Each of us has been hurt by someone whom we have loved, trusted, or admired. A friend told me that his girlfriend cheated on him with his best friend. It was such a painful experience for him. He has moved on since, but he doubts if he will ever be as trusting of anyone again. This was affecting his current relationship, and he knew he was not giving his best due to his past experience.

In reality, not everyone who reminds you of a painful past experience will inflict pain upon you. Because your loved one cheated on you does not make every potential lover a cheat. It is unwise to allow the past to direct the future. Rather, let it serve as a guide.

Allowing your past to direct you is like looking through the rearview mirror while driving. It is only a matter of time until you crash. Learn the lessons of the past, and forget the details. To move on, you need to look at the future with a bias-free lens. Bringing past hurts into current relationships will only cause dissatisfaction. It is difficult, but you must let go of the past so you can experience a fulfilling relationship.

What Your Wardrobe and Library Says About You

If I saw your wardrobe, I could tell who you are, but when I see your library, I can tell who you will become.

I was watching a business report on Cable News Network (CNN) about the current unemployment rate in America. The analysis showed that there was a wide gap in the unemployment rate between people with a college or higher degree and those without. The current unemployment rate for those with higher education was less than five percent while those without were in the double digits. This shows that the skills required for current and future jobs require advanced or specialized skills. Simply put, you earn what you learn.

Some people mortgage their future by focusing only on the present. When you spend all your money on clothes and things rather than investing in your education or trade, you are probably mortgaging your future. Where you put your money is a good indicator of your passion and goals. When you invest in your passion, the returns will enable you to enjoy the perks of life.

Are your daily actions drawing you toward or away from your goals? What new information are you gathering that will help you achieve your goals or have that competitive advantage? How much of your resources are you investing into your passion? It is crucial that you update yourself with the latest technology or information pertinent to your interests and the world around you.

Yesterday's papers belong in the trash bin. Likewise, your education or experience may become irrelevant in the future. Get updated in order to not become outdated in your career. Learn new things, take a class, or go back to school.

A Loss Can Be a Blessing in Disguise

Always remind yourself that whoever walks out on you did not deserve you and is not connected to your future. (Of course, this is assuming you were not the cause of someone leaving you.) Like my parents used to say, a broken engagement is better than a broken marriage. It is a blessing to lose someone before the stakes are really high and the consequences even more so. It is their loss to not appreciate a diamond when they see one.

I have had people I loved and valued walk out on me, and those were hurting times. However, I must confess that in hindsight some of these "walk outs" were blessings in disguise. They made me stronger and wiser and taught me to believe in myself.

Sometimes it is appropriate for someone to walk out on us to snap us back to reality and save us from destruction. Many addicts seek help only when a loved one threatens to leave or actually walks out the door. In an abusive relationship, the person who is being abused is better off without the abuser. Hopefully, this will serve as a wake-up call for the abuser to seek help.

Great Packaging is Never Enough

You may never get a chance to make a second impression so make the first one count. There is no doubt that the packaging of a product conveys a lot of information to the potential buyer. Apple has excellent packaging for its products, and in my opinion, gives it an edge over similar brands. No matter how well packaged a product is though, the real question is whether it can meet and even exceed expectations.

There is an important lesson we can learn from great packaging. Can you imagine someone going for an interview at a bank wearing flip-flops, a tee shirt, and a pair of shorts? No matter how talented that person is, a wall has already gone up in the minds of the interviewers. Great packaging gets you noticed and will open doors for you. What keeps those doors from closing is your performance and attitude. Make sure your content matches your advertising. Focus more on your character, and your reputation will take care of itself.

A Lizard in Africa Is a Lizard in America

I spent most of my life in a developing country that lacked basic infrastructure; healthcare, electricity, water, and good roads were not the norm. Having electricity for up to ten hours a day was cause for celebration. As a result of these living conditions, some people in developing countries have attributed living abroad as an end to all their problems.

I have had the opportunity to study in England and the United States and have discovered that all that glitters is not gold. Likewise, many people hope that when they get a better job or move to another school, neighborhood, city, or country their lives will change for the better. Little do they know that when the grass appears greener on the other side, it may only be an indication to water or fertilize their own lawn.

While it is true that some geographical locations offer better opportunities for its citizenry, success is a heart thing. I have seen poverty even in the richest countries of the world. I have met lawyers, doctors, and bankers who have left their home countries only to become cab drivers in the West.

If you can succeed in the worst of times and places, you can succeed anywhere. Your potential is not necessarily dependent on where you are geographically but a thing of the heart. No person, place, or situation can determine what you can or cannot do unless you allow him, her, or it to do so. You can make your world a palace or a prison. If you are hardworking, creative, and determined, you will succeed anywhere. Make it happen where you are. The answer does not always lie in relocating.

Get In or Get Out

In my opinion, the most frustrating individuals to work with are people who play it safe. They are neither high achievers nor underperformers; they enjoy coasting.

People who play it safe do not make significant contributions and eventually drain the team because they have no opinion other than that of the group. Make a decision today to be fully in or fully out of whatever group you are in. The people who suffer first are usually the people in the middle of the road. Stand up for something; you are a voice, not an echo. Speak up, and be heard. You have substance, so make it count.

Admit When You Don't Know Something

Any time I encounter fuzzy questions, I tell my students I don't know the answer but I will get back to them in the next class period. In the past, I had come up with answers that I later found out were wrong. I did this because I feared my students would lose respect for me if I didn't have all the answers. I later found that students lost respect for an instructor when he came across as infallible.

John Maxwell says, "A man must be big enough to admit his mistakes, smart enough to profit from them, and strong enough to correct them[10]." No one is a custodian of knowledge, and no individual has all the answers. People can tell when you are unsure of or not prepared for something, so it is a good idea to get it out in the open. After all, you are only telling them what they already know. In the words of Lao Tzu, "The wise man is one who knows what he does not know."

Only You Can Solve Your Problem

Only you can solve your problem. The buck stops at your table. People can counsel you, but you must make the final call. Counsel should never become a permanent crutch. There is a time to get advice from others, and there is a time to act. No one can nor should do it but you. You are the one in the situation, and no one knows it better than you. You are qualified to make that choice if you make an informed decision. When you realize that you are the master of your faith and the captain of your ship and that God is the wind beneath your sails, you are destined to succeed.

Indecisiveness wastes time and resources. C.S. Lewis said that "We all want progress, but if you're on the wrong road, progress means doing an about-turn and walking back to the right road; in that case, the man who turns back soonest is the most progressive". Do not be a professional leftover addict who just waits to get the crumbs under the table. It is not wise to schedule your life on other people's calendars by expecting them to make things happen for you. Take responsibility for your actions. The time to act is now. You have waited long enough.

Self-Made Person ... Seriously?

Have you heard the phrase "Self-made person"? This statement is inaccurate because no person is an island, and when you dig deep into successful people's stories, you will discover someone helped them along the way. George Mattew Adam says, "There is no such thing as a self-made man, we are all made of thousands of others[9]". Every successful person at some point in their life has had to stand on the shoulder of others to succeed.

A captain has the map for the journey, but to get there, he needs a solid crew. The captain knows that tempests may come, and he would need a team to weather through the stormy waters. So when you say you are self-made, you are actually taking all the credit for your success and watering down the efforts of your crew members.

Great leaders, sport coaches, entertainers, actors, and directors all acknowledge it took a team to make their dreams come true. Who are your crew members? Do you value and recognize their contributions? Any time you say you are self-made, you make their contributions insignificant.

Power Talk

How you start your day determines the rest of your day. What are the first words that go through your mind when you wake up in the morning? Rather than leave the day to chance, why don't you take charge by having a power talk?

I start by thanking God for the opportunity to witness and for all the opportunities He will give me that day. A portion of my power talk goes like this, "I have what it takes to go through the day without getting ruffled. I am victorious in life. I am treasure, not trash. I am a problem solver. I meet needs. I make things happen for others. I look for ways to be a blessing for others. I am cool, calm, and collected." Power talk is how I condition myself for the day, and it starts me off on the right note, supercharged and excited.

You may have your power talk when you exercise, eat breakfast, or drive to work. Set your day by your words before someone else does.

The Best Man Does Not Always Win

A sad fact of life is that the best man, candidate, or team does not always win. Take a look at sport tournaments, especially the finals, and you will see several instances of this phenomenon. A noteworthy example is the miracle on ice hockey story of 1980.

The Olympic hockey game between the United States and Russia is regarded as one of the greatest upsets in sports history. The match was between the amateur US team and the professional Russian team. The US team was the underdog going into this game, but they ended up beating the Russians with the score 4–3.

What made the difference for the US team was opportunity. The person or team that makes the best use of the opportunities available to them will always come out on top. The US team had sixteen shots on goal while the Russians had thirty-nine shots. The distinction was that the US team used their chances well.

It takes more than hard work or talent to succeed. You must seek out and make the best use of opportunities available to you.

Go Further and Achieve Greater

I have discovered that when relating to loved ones, I get the best results when I go the extra mile they don't expect. This catches them off guard, and they end the duel. Anyone and everyone can do the ordinary, but those who do the extraordinary never experience traffic on the road leading to people's hearts.

It takes strength and courage to do what you don't want to do, but that might be what is necessary to get the desired outcome. Albert Einstein says it best, "Insanity: doing the same thing over and over again and expecting different results". If you want to achieve a better outcome then do the little extra.

Make Your Setback a Comeback

Gold is an attractive and valuable metal. In order for gold to be pure, it must be refined in a furnace, a process that separates impurities from the gold. Likewise, in our lives, tough times can serve as a refining process for us that builds our character, develops our perseverance, and makes us better people in the long run.

I do not know of any great person who has not had a major setback in his or her life. The major difference between a great person and an ordinary one is their perspective. Great people throughout history have always used their darkest moments as positive turning points in their lives. Other people allow the dark times to control and direct the rest of their lives. They become victims of their situation and remain boxed in but great people see challenges as an opportunity to try new things.

Are you going through a difficult time? Remember, great things are birthed in the midst of trying times.

Every Dream Has a Price Tag

Steve Jobs, Steve Wozniak, and Ronald Wayne are the founders of Apple Computers (now Apple, Inc.). Jobs and Wozniak sold their possessions to start the company in a garage. There was no guarantee that it was going to become the success it is today, but they believed in their product and put their money where their heart was.

What is your dream? What are you ready to sacrifice to make it a reality? Every dream has a price tag and is called a dream for a reason. You cannot hold onto the old and expect to receive the new at the same time. You may need to give something up to get ahead. I challenge you to walk away from mediocrity and from settling for second best. It is never too late to get on the right path. Susan Boyles became famous when she decided to walk away from self-doubt and worries about age and what people would think of her. She was a contestant on *Britain's Got Talent*, and it paid off. Her song "I Dreamed a Dream" made Susan a worldwide singing sensation.

Do Not Envy What You Want to Become

Have you ever envied something or someone? I have. But I learned from my mother not to envy the success of others. It is important to realize that envy is an emotion over which you can have an upper hand.

In graduate school, when my friends talked about the success of their experiments when mine was rock bottom, I often inquired of them how they achieved their success. I learned from my peers and chose to celebrate with them. I did not dismiss them or look for an excuse to belittle their achievements. I always treated them the way I wanted to be treated when I was successful. I eventually had my own success, and it felt great.

Use Your Two Memories Wisely

I have noticed a pattern in some of my "book smart" friends who have photographic memories. This quality that helps them excel in their careers also has the potential to ruin them when it comes to interpersonal relationships. Some of them find it difficult to let go of setbacks, hurts, and negative past experiences. They hold grudges, which inevitably makes them bitter. On the other hand, I have noticed some of my other friends put past experiences in their short-term memory and are much happier.

Use your long-term memory for positive experiences and to envision success and your short-term memory for setbacks and negative experiences. No wonder Jesus said in Mattew 18:3, "I tell you the truth, unless you change and become like little children, you will never enter the kingdom of heaven. Children get over hurtful situations quickly, which is almost unbelievable.

An Idea Is Not Good Enough

It takes more than talent to succeed. Many people have ideas, but few work on them. Of all those ideas, one person or company usually gets the credit.

Steve Jobs was not the first person to have the idea of carrying your whole music album in your pocket, but he was the first to make everyone want the product. Having a great product is half of the equation for success, and marketing is the other half. Steve Jobs had both, which explains why Apple is the most profitable company in America today. Likewise, there have been several other social networking sites before Facebook, but Facebook is the name we remember today.

Having an idea and working on it is not good enough. You must determine how to make people desire your product. The *New York Times* bestseller list is not a best writer list. If marketing is not your strength, partner with someone who is good at it.

Geography and Your Success Story

I now use a smartphone, so I am connected 24/7, which is pretty convenient. To enjoy the full benefits of my phone, I joined a cellular network with wide coverage. Likewise, you might have talent and ideas, but you have to be in a place that encourages and develops your creativity as I had to change my cellular network to get the best out of my phone.

Similarly, have you ever wondered what happens to the moon and the stars during the day? They appear at night, but they are also there during the day. We don't see them because the sun outshines them. The only difference between a shining star and an unnoticed star is timing. Likewise, you may need to relocate, change jobs, have a paradigm shift, or be creative (create a YouTube video, go online with your business, or rebrand yourself) in order for your gifts and talents to shine. Success is not just hard work but working smartly as well. According to a CNN banner, "Smart is the new rich."

Push Yourself

Personal trainers or coaches take you through a series of exercises increasing in intensity until you reach your maximum. From the information he gathers from your performance, he gives you a working range of weights for your exercise.

The only way to know your limits is to push yourself to your highest level. You cannot eyeball your potential. Have you ever met someone who said he could not do or achieve something even though he had never tried it before? That is mediocre.

A rubber band's potential is in the stretching. Get into the arena, and make an attempt. You never know what's in you until you try.

Limits Do Not Have to Be Permanent

There was a time in my life when I struggled with weight issues, so I joined a group of friends who jogged regularly. My first few attempts were terrible; I stopped every two minutes, and it seemed really hard. However, one particular friend stayed with me while the others went ahead, and that encouraged me to press on. After two months, I was able to go three miles without stopping. Through persistence, I overcame my initial limitations.

We all have things we are not good at, but rather than letting it stay that way, we can get more information about the subject, take a class, or ask for help. Do not accept the status quo. You can improve. I enjoy playing tennis; I am certainly not Wimbledon material, but I keep getting better by practicing often.

Practice makes permanent. Keep at it.

Get a Mentor

As a scientist, your starting point for a project is not to reinvent the wheel. Instead, you gather a lot of information about the project, find out what had been done before, why it was done, and what the outcome was. Equipped with this knowledge, you are better informed about the areas you can make a contribution. Likewise, in our lives, there are people who have gone ahead of us who have information that can help us. We don't have to waste time reinventing the wheel either.

Any time I want to make a significant purchase, the first thing I do is find out the quality of the merchandise from people who have bought the product. When I travel, I ask friends for the best hotels with the lowest rates and where the interesting spots are. All this is to ensure that I receive good value for my money and time and thus minimize my loss.

Likewise, life is a journey. Some people have been where you want to go. Why don't you ask them for advice? There is no excuse these days to not have a mentor. Mentorship is something you pursue. Potential mentors are all around via the Internet, books, and face-to–face meetings. It is important you choose mentors based on their reputation and who have a belief system similar to yours.

Knowledge Is Only Powerful When Applied

Information can be powerful. It separates the reformed from the deformed and the conformed from the transformed. We are living in the technology age, and it is vital to stay informed to be up to par with society. In our personal lives, many people pay less attention to being informed about the people in their lives and the world around them.

Information can make an ugly situation better and a good situation great. Isaac Newton, considered to be one of the greatest scientists who ever lived, discovered his laws of motion when he saw an apple drop from a tree. His childlike curiosity and quest for knowledge made him wonder why an apple dropped perpendicular to the ground.

Seek information from mentors, books, friends, pastors, and colleagues and do something with it.

Integrity Makes You Valuable

Children are the future of our country, and it is vital they have people in their lives they can look up to.

When I moved to California from England, I had a bit of a culture shock. I discovered that when some people said one thing, it meant another. There were some occasions when I invited people over, and their response was, "Sure, we will be there." But they never showed up or indicated they would be absent. A friend later told me that many Californians will not say they won't show up because they don't want to hurt you. I was told that if they were going to attend a function, they would ask for more specifics.

I was raised to take people at their word. Double talk was strange to me. So I can imagine how confused kids become when their parents' words are not consistent with their actions. We need to deeply reflect about the future of our nation for the upcoming generation.

One thing that is scarce these days is people with integrity. It may be easier to find a needle in a haystack than to find a few good men. The government and religious leaders have failed this test over and over again with all the scandals in the media. The culture of, "Say what you mean and mean what you say" seems to be a thing of the past. People are no longer accountable for their actions and pass the buck.

Integrity is so rare these days that a person who possesses it is not only desirable but praiseworthy. Are you a person of integrity? Make a commitment today.

Do Not Fix Your Weaknesses

The natural human tendency is to either hide our weaknesses or spend enormous time and energy trying to fix them. We have all heard that a chain is only as strong as its weakest link, but that does not apply to every situation. In fact, a study performed by the Gallup organization in the book *Now Discover Your Strengths* by Marcus Buckingham and Donald O. Clifton showed that the most successful people were not all well-rounded but were successful because they paid more attention to their strengths than their weaknesses. Buckingham and Clifton suggest managing our weaknesses by getting more information, creating a support system for ourselves, or seeking help. For example, if you had a tough time learning math like I did while growing up, the way to improve is to study more and get tutored on the subject.

There are times when improving your weakness may be important to fulfilling your dream. For example, if you got a D in both math and music and desire to be an engineer, your priority would be to improve your math deficiency. Since the music grade would not have any impact on your future career, investing a lot of time on that may not be the wisest decision. Please don't get me wrong; I support people being the best in whatever they do. I am simply advocating that we make life choices based on our strengths.

Having a Dream Is Not Good Enough

Many people, like me, have at some point in their lives dreamed of winning a million dollars through the lottery. I recently heard of a person who won over a half-*billion* dollars. I found myself daydreaming and planning how I would invest the money if it were me who had won it.

What is interesting is that some people who won the lottery often ended up poorer than they were before. Jack Whittaker was the president of a successful contracting firm with a net worth of over a million dollars. He took home a cash price of $113.4 million dollars, but four years later, Jack was struggling financially. Many others are in similar situations where they walked into a dream they were not prepared for. Winning was not the problem; it was what they did with what they had that ruined them. These people obviously had no financial planning or goals beyond their current situation.

In victory or defeat, there is always the next step, which I believe is most important because it can sustain your victory, keep you complacent, or drop you to a lower level than where you started. Many of us have great dreams, but in reality, I think they are only wishful thinking if we don't make adequate preparations. I wonder what Jack Whittaker's story might have been if he had a financial adviser help him manage his wealth. Jack said if he could do it all over again he would not have played the lottery. I believe his and many others' story could have had different endings. Having a dream is great and preparing for it is better, but having a solid plan when the dream becomes a reality is success.

Do you know that success itself can be a hindrance? When you become content in your victories and accolades, you risk the danger of becoming complacent. Discontent is what drives you to do better and be better and is what drives and sustains innovation. What about your career and relationship dreams? We learn from Jack that living only in the moment is not the best way to go.,There is a British Army adage that says "Proper preparation prevents poor performance." So what are you waiting for? Start preparing today.

America's Lost Treasure: Gratitude

I received a thank you and a gift card from a former student whom I taught over summer. She really didn't have to buy me a card much less a gift card, as she had already thanked me in person several times. But her gesture made me examine the art of gratitude.

I believe true gratitude is not just a convenient thing you say or do on the spot but is something that is well thought out. You know that kind gestures bestowed on you are those that others choose to make. I am guessing you say thank you to someone at least once a day. But do you really mean it or is it just another phrase?

Many people have lost the art of gratitude for the things they have, the country they live in, their freedom of choice, their health, and the list goes on and on. People have developed a sense of entitlement, thinking they deserve what they have or is being done for them. Friend, you really need to check out what is going on in other countries and be grateful for what you have.

Don't let the anxiety of future expectations dampen the joys of the present. The truth is, things could be worse. You could have been born in a poverty-stricken or war-torn country or perhaps under a bridge, but you live in America, the greatest country on Earth. You can choose your friends, but not your family. So always be thankful. Your life is a gift from above.

Major in Your Talents, Minor in Your Interests

I supervised a chemistry laboratory session, and it was my custom to chat with the students about their motivations for the class. One of my students said she was undecided about what she wanted to really do. On further inquiry, she said she had a lot of things she was interested in, but she wanted to be certain before making a lifetime commitment. Her mother had a PhD in biochemistry from Stanford and a good job, but she left it all to become a full-time artist because her high-paying job frustrated her and she wanted to do what had always brought her joy.

I then understood what my student meant by "really do." We often see people major in their interests and take their talents and gifting for granted. The reasons range from security to family expectations to just not believing in themselves and their talents. The result is, people play it safe and usually end up unfulfilled and full of regret. It is a choice we need to make hopefully earlier in our journey than later.

Brown or Burned Out?

There always seems to be one person who carries the burden in a relationship. He or she always bends over backward and always loves, forgives, cares, and is available while the other party in the relationship just goes with the flow. The person who always initiates eventually gets frustrated because the responsibility for the relationship is one-sided. A relationship that started out exciting and promising now feels like a task.

It is important that both parties contribute to the relationship. You can't blame the passive person for not contributing, if you never really allowed him or her to contribute because you had it covered all the time. When two people take a journey together, they will definitely move at different paces. To ensure that neither party gets burned out, you must create a rhythm that ensures happiness for both and that the weight is not unduly on one person.

Playing It Safe Could Cost Your Life

Looking back, people who achieved great things were individuals who faced their fears and perceived limitations. They saw possibilities and opportunities where others saw mountains and brick walls.

People who play it safe live average lives. They are barely one step ahead of others in the rat race and just hang in the balance, not in the red but not above board either. "Play-it-safers" merely exist; they are not living.

You are worth more than you think and deserve to live life to the fullest. To move to the next level, you must decide where you would rather be.

The Power of a Second Opinion

Following your gut instinct is safe, asking for a second opinion is safer, but considering others' thoughts before making a decision is safest. Success is knowing when to follow your instincts, ask for a second opinion, or make an informed decision based on the advice of others.

Proverbs 20:18, New Living Translation says, "Plans succeed through good counsel; don't go to war without wise advice." One thing is certain: Getting counsel from people who are relevant, objective, and knowledgeable when making life-changing decisions is surely a great idea.

Shortcuts Can Shorten Your Success

People who try to jump to the top seem to get there quicker, but they also fall down faster than people who climb to the top. I am sure you have heard different versions of that saying before, but I think there is something missing from that saying: the phrase "at the beginning." There are many ways to get to the top in life: the slow and steady path, an inheritance, and shady, get-rich-quick schemes. Depending on how quickly you want a return, the first two ways are slow while the third way (the "will do anything to make it" path) is much quicker. Short cuts may get you to the top quicker but they shorten your life span there. However, if history is anything to go by, success is like a ladder, and it takes time to climb to the top.

“Me-Time” Moments

It always starts in front of the mirror, all the singing, admiring yourself, and pep talks you give yourself. These “me-time” moments are invaluable because they are your backstage preparations where you build your confidence, mess up, redesign, and rebuild yourself. These times prepare you for the opportunities that will arrive on your doorstep.

Melanie Amaro, the 2011 winner of X Factor USA, was always practicing, rehearsing, singing in church, or holding her hairbrush as a microphone in front of the mirror. When the competition came to the United States, she was ready, as she had spent the last eighteen years of her life preparing. So make hay when the sun shines.

Are You a Crossover?

Crossovers are people who have succeeded in their chosen careers despite all odds. They are pacesetters with local content but broad impact. One of the greatest crossovers of our time is President Barack Obama, the first African American president of the greatest nation on Earth. He was not political aristocracy and had only a few years under his belt in politics. He did not look the part or have the experience people believed a president of the United States should have. Few people thought he stood a chance. But Barack Obama had a dream and hope in his heart and gave voice to his intention by taking a bold step. The rest is history.

Who is writing the story of your life? Who is carving out your destiny? Do you see the obstacles or the opportunities? Are you battling with, "It has never been done before"? Obama was a first in many regards, and you can be too. When you think of a computer, who comes to mind? Bill Gates, Steve Jobs, and Michael Dell. When you think of phones, I am sure you think of the iPhone. In the entertainment industry, few artists of color have been able to cross all divides. Celebrities like Denzel Washington, Michael Jackson, Whitney Houston, Beyoncé, Naomi Campbell, Rihanna, Jamie Foxx, and Halle Berry are referred to as crossovers, as they have overcome stereotypes and appeal to mainstream audiences all over the world. One thing they have in common is they create or make great use of opportunities. They are exceptionally gifted and have taken huge risks.

To be a crossover, you must find what you are really good at and give it your all. One day, the kaleidoscope will move in your direction, and you will have your opportunity.

“I Will Be Ready in August”

These were one of the last words of Whitney Houston to her mentor, friend, and record label boss, Clive Davis. Michael Jackson was preparing for his “This Is It” concert. Unfortunately, both artists were not able to experience what they desired in their hearts.

Your goal or aspiration may be achieved later or sooner than August. You are only guaranteed today; tomorrow is a gift, so make the most of today by giving it your best. If you don’t get tomorrow, you have the satisfaction of knowing you have given today your all.

My mom and I had a misunderstanding the week she went to heaven. Fortunately for me, we reconciled, but I do not know how I would be able to live with myself if we had not settled our misunderstanding beforehand. If you need to mend a broken relationship, break a habit, lose weight, or be the best you can be, today is all you have. Make it count because tomorrow may be too late.

Intentionality Determines Functionality

Kerri Allyson Strug became a household name during the Olympics at Atlanta in 1996. Kerri won a gold medal in the pole vault event despite having an injured ankle. It was serious because her coach had to carry her to the podium. Kerri did not go to the Olympics just to attend but she went to compete and win. Her drive kept her going despite her frail health.

Simply put, you need to take responsibility for your success, happiness, ideas, thoughts, and creativity. No one can make anything happen but you. You need to be intentional and proactive; make that phone call, submit your manuscript, or launch your business. Kerri did not allow her feelings determine her actions during the Olympics.

Your intentionality can be contagious and draw others to your cause. Your passion for your product or dream will attract like-minded people. It is great to get a second opinion, but that is what it is, a *second* opinion. Do not let other people's opinions become your facts. Second opinions are great guides but should not be the final authority.

So what are you waiting for? Just do it! Nothing works until you work it.

Fever Is a Symptom, Not the Problem

I am sure you recall when you or someone you love had a fever. The world slowed down as you languished in discomfort and pain. My first instinct when I have a fever is to grab Tylenol. I remember a particular occasion when my one-year-old son had a fever. We gave him Tylenol, which worked for a while, but the fever came back. We eventually took him to the hospital and found he had an ear infection. The fever was a symptom of the ear infection. The medication was not addressing the problem, and so it was not effective. Likewise, when we are going through issues in our lives, it is tempting to try to fix the symptoms without addressing the problem. We need to dig below the surface to find out what the real problem is and then deal with it. This will ensure that we do not have a recurrence.

Guard Your Heart

On February 11, 2012, at 3.55 p.m. Pacific Standard Time, Whitney Houston was pronounced dead at age forty-eight. She was a global superstar and a singing wonder. She was referred to as "The Voice," as her voice was a God-given gift. Whitney was the yardstick by which other upcoming artists were measured. She proved that music is indeed the universal language. Her songs were classics and relevant to people of all ages. My favorite is "The Greatest Love of All." Unfortunately, Whitney had her troubles as well, which later affected her career. Many people have claimed that a lot of Whitney's problems could be traced to her troubled marriage. In the movie *The BodyGuard*, Kevin Costner was able to protect her from an assassin's bullet, but in reality, nobody could protect her from the people she loved. The key, my friend, is to guard your heart so you don't let just anyone in. An initial strong connection or attraction to someone should not automatically grant them entry into your life. You need to take things slow—time will reveal people's true intentions.

Your Difference Makes You Beautiful

As a kid, I wondered how McDonald's and Burger King could be next door to each other and still remain in business. But as I grew up, I realized that their only common denominator was food. Their products were different, and as a result, they attracted distinct customers. This gave me the confidence to be myself and to not try to blend in with the crowd.

What makes you different makes you beautiful. Your uniqueness distinguishes you from the rest of the group. It is important you realize that your difference makes you attractive. You must be comfortable with and celebrate your peculiarity. Know deep down that you are important and have the potential to be a part of the solution wherever you are. Think about it. What is the point of hiring two people with the same set of skills in the same office?

Variety is the spice of life. You are a contributor, and you are valuable.

Mistakes Are Good

We are imperfect people living in an imperfect world. We have all made mistakes and will all make mistakes in the future. But mistakes can be positive when we have learned from them and have matured in the process. Most of us think of mistakes as setbacks and dread making them. The problem with this approach is that it could limit us to our comfort zone. Nothing new or great is discovered in safety. Making mistakes does not make us a failure; rather they are often opportunities for growth.

Making a mistake is okay. Even making the same mistake twice is forgivable. But making it a third time is plain ignorance. You are not learning from your experiences and this could cost you a lot. For example, anyone who wants to study medicine has to pass some required examinations. Without a pass grade, he or she would not have the requirements to continue studying medicine. Now imagine that person taking an exam on the same subject three times. This tells me that he or she has not developed the strategy for studying and then passing the exam. I do not believe it means the person is incapable of getting an A but rather that the individual has not learned what he or she is doing wrong.

When situations do not go as planned in our lives, it is easy to blame everyone but ourselves. The problem with this attitude is that we stay longer in the pit of ignorance. Albert Einstein defines insanity as doing the same thing and expecting a different result. When I have tried solving a problem numerous times and have received the same results, I usually change my strategy by seeking help or doing further research.

You don't have to be perfect; no one is. Mistakes can be the building blocks of your success story. So the next time you slip up, ask yourself, "What can I learn from this experience?"

Moving Forward: The Little Things Matter

Stolen

I am the little girl stolen
The boy taken from his home
The girl who lived next door
The boy who you saw in the park
This is our story:

They came in the night
Tore me from my mothers arms
I cried, "Daddy! Daddy!" but no one came—I must not be worth it
They forced their fist across my crown
Knocking it to the ground, I followed it
On the ground I curled, stripped bare
Crying and screaming, as they kicked me
With their words, they stripped me of all my worth

I am beaten and bruised
My bones are broken
I no longer fight back, for my will is stolen
My lips have been sealed
All hope has been crushed
Threats of murder of those I love
If a mistake I should make

In chains I lie trapped in their grasp
They inject their poisons into my veins
My mind numb to pain as my body festers and bleeds

I'm no longer alive, merely there

Your neighbor rents me for his pleasure
In the closet I fulfill his vile lusts
I no longer care
For my dreams are gone
They force me to work
In the heat I labor for you
So you can buy cheap

I am no longer me
I am now their slave
I am stolen
I am trapped
I am their slave
I am their worthless slave
If only one could come and save
But no one comes for me
If only I was worth it
If only there was an escape
If only one could take me away
But there is none
For you sit on your couch watching TV
As I waste away

—John M. Barry

John showed me his poem after Sunday service. I really like it, as it brings to light people all around us who are hurting from the pain of the past. Some have been physically abused, emotionally broken, and have suffered through traumatic experiences. Their worth and dignity has been stolen from them, and they are scarred for life.

The good news is that we can reach out to others and be a light to them by helping and praying with them. We can't fix them, but we can show them we care, which is where healing begins.

Living in the past gives our future to our captors, but living a life of forgiveness gives us freedom. There is always hope. Our best days are ahead of us.

Crisp or Worn Dollar Bill, Same Purchasing Power

A worn out dollar bill is still valuable. It can purchase everything like a crisp dollar bill (ignore the vending machine). Likewise, regardless of your past experiences, you are still valuable. Your past may have left you broken, wounded, and worn out, but you can still have a comeback.

Reach within and bring out those qualities that make you unique. Do not let anyone define you or put you in a box. Hollywood has defined the perfect look, and many people have bought into the deception. We forget the industry is all about make-believe.

You are as beautiful or ugly as you feel. You have strengths that make you adorable and are admirable. Why not focus on what you have and not on what you wish you had? Gifted people are those who use their gifts, so discover yours and begin to use them. When you do, you glow and that reveals your inner beauty.

Regardless of your history, you are still precious. It is time for your comeback. Let go of anything or anyone who makes you feel unworthy.

Scars versus Open Wounds

Scars are good reminders of the past. They can be touched without your feeling any pain, unlike wounds, which cause you to relive the pain.

Two days into our vacation, a hair stylist accidentally poured boiling water on my wife. As a result, my wife could do nothing while we were on vacation because of her incredible pain. The doctor told her to leave the burnt area uncovered as much as possible. Day after day, week after week, the pain reduced, the wound started healing, and she slowly returned to her daily routine.

Likewise, when we live in the past, we reopen those wounds that cripple us and keep us from functioning at our peak. Let bygones be bygones, and let the old wounds heal. My wife's wound had to be exposed to the air to aid the healing process. In order for you and I to heal from our past wounds, we need to bring our emotional pain into the open. That open air is forgiveness. We may need to talk with or lovingly confront someone. Lastly, we need to forgive ourselves.

Face Value

Do people get what they see when they get to know you? Or are you like a chameleon that blends into the environment? Have you ever met people whose first impressions were scripted? I once had a classmate who was not very sociable even when people tried to make friends with him. We both attended an assessment interview, and to my surprise, he was the most charismatic and enthusiastic person. Friendly and most caring, he reached out to people during the interview and was able to fool the interviewers during that brief period.

You may be able to fool people some of the time, but you cannot fool people all of the time. Your character can be likened to fumes. No matter how much you try to contain them, they will always escape. The real you does not have to be rehearsed. True beauty comes from within though it may take awhile for people to see it. When they do, you become a rare gem in their eyes. Your character glistens like the facets of a ruby, and that makes you unique.

Don't hide your inner beauty. You have something special no one else can offer.

Don't Wait for Permission to Be Yourself

The only permission you need to be yourself has already been given to you just by being on Earth. I discovered that in some areas of my life I was unconsciously waiting for permission or others' approval to be myself or to take some action. I was so focused on what people would think about me, and that put me in a box, which was frustrating and depressing. I later discovered that the more I was myself and stopped seeking approval, the happier I became and the more people liked me. Being myself makes my day, and that makes someone else's day.

True Colors

What does "True colors" really mean? It means your individuality, who you really are and how you express your originality. To show your true colors, you must be true to yourself. True colors can be influenced by your environment, experiences, background, and genetics.

It is important that you understand how your environment can cast a shadow on your true colors. I have a friend who grew up in a polygamous home, and survival was based on how well versed he was in family politics and his ability to get on with members of his extended family. His background has had a profound influence on who he is. He is guarded emotionally and has become a diplomat when expressing his true feelings.

You may have picked up some characteristics, traits, and beliefs while growing up, and it is important you know why you act the way you do. This knowledge will help you distinguish the traits developed as a result of your environment from your intrinsic nature, which are your true colors. A person who knows his true colors is a person who is in touch with himself.

You know you are not perfect. You mess up at times, and your imperfections are not a permanent. But despite your flaws and weaknesses, you know you are still valuable. To be true to yourself, you need to realize that you are a work in progress. Depending on where you are on your journey, you may need to wear a caution sign so you don't mess other people up while dealing with your own issues.

True colors, like I mentioned earlier, are dependent on genetics, environment, life experiences, background, etc. For a moment, let's picture a five-year-old wearing a white outfit playing soccer on the field with his friends. Imagine what his clothes will look like when he returns home. They may have turned brown or green from dirt on the field. So what color would you say is the *true* color of boy's clothing? The true color would be the color before he played soccer.

If we can apply this example to our lives, we start out excited about life and what it has to offer, but as time passes, we fall into the mud of life and get stained with lies, abuse, loss, rejection, and betrayal. The sad reality is that unlike the stains on the little boy's clothing, which was temporary, many of us have been stained in numerous ways and have allowed those stains to become a part of who we are. The stains ended up being permanent because we became bitter and chose not to engage in that arena of life gain. We allowed our past hurts to control and direct us.

There is good news, though. Those stains do not have to be permanent; we can choose to launder them. In my opinion and experience, the best laundry detergent for any hurt is forgiveness. A good place to start is talking to people you trust, such as a family member, counselor, pastor, or friend so the healing can begin.

Quality Customer Service

Do you work to impress others, or is excelling at what you do second nature to you? I worked in a clothing store on the weekends while studying in England and received commission for every store card I opened. I discovered I had a tendency to show preferential treatment to people based on their appearance. Many of the people I thought would be approved based on their appearance actually were declined, and the people I least expected actually got accepted. This taught me to never size people up based on what they look like.

I remember a scene from the movie *Pretty Woman* when Julia Roberts was told to leave a store on Rodeo Drive because she did not fit the profile of the person who typically shopped there. Although she had a lot of money to spend, the sales associate missed it because Julia did not fit the profile.

The quality of customer service should be the same irrespective of whom you are attending to. Think about it. People you consider to be nobody today could be great tomorrow. Always treat people based on who they can be and never on who you think they are.

There Is a Hero Inside You

If you look in your heart, you will see that a hero lies inside you, as the lyrics from Mariah Carey's song "Hero" says.

I was moved by the story of nine-year-old Rachel Beckweth who died shortly after trying to raise three hundred dollars for fifteen people in need of clean water. Rachel wanted to give back to a needy society on her birthday. She was not interested in receiving bicycles and charm bracelets, which most nine-year-old girls would love as presents. Instead, she wanted to provide clean water to people, so she requested that friends and family donate money to a fundraising page she created through Charity Water. Thankfully, Rachel's dream was fulfilled and lives on.

Whose life are you impacting today? Heroes are not free of problems themselves, but they know there is greater joy in helping others than just living in a tiny bubble called Me. Someone needs something that you have, you are an answer to someone's prayer. Who are you going to be a blessing to today?

When Signs Go Up, People Show Up

I remember the excitement I felt when the Nugget store was opening a block from my house. Anticipation first occurred when the "Coming Soon" signs went up. When the store finally opened for business, as expected happy shoppers like me were there to welcome the store.

In front of most stores is an open or closed sign depending on their business hours. When the open sign is up, people show up to do business. You would not expect people to come to your store if you have a closed sign on the door either on purpose or by accident. Likewise, in our lives we have a sign we put up that either draws people to us or pushes them away from us. If you find yourself alone or lonely, ask yourself, "What sign am I putting up that is visible to my customers?"

The signs you put up consciously or unconsciously are directly related to your thoughts and how you perceive yourself. If you think you are special and a treasure, people who come to you will treat you as such. If you believe you are not any good or that the people who love you are doing you a favor, you may attract abusive people into your life. So, friend, you may want to take a close look at the people who always show up to connect with you. This is a good indicator of the type of signals you are transmitting to others about yourself.

Choose, Be Chosen, or Be Left Behind

Many people are waiting for the right person to notice all their stellar qualities and approach them. This reminds me of the mating season of mammals. The males must prepare a lot to be noticed and desired by the opposite sex. If the female likes what she sees, she gives a green signal to the dominant male. The problem with this approach when relating to people is that a lot of people are shy and wait to be approached by others. So everybody is waiting for somebody, and then nobody does anything. The other downside is that people rarely get what they want because they are not going for it. They expect the other person to read their minds.

If you don't choose and are then chosen, you feel unfulfilled. You wonder why you are always behind on the things that are important to you. If you wait for people to come to you, eternity may not be long enough. Go after what you want.

Dry Fish Is Difficult to Straighten

We eat some really good traditional fish in Nigeria. We curve it round a stick, dry and then roast it. If you try to straighten the fish, it might break because it has become brittle.

Like the dry fish, some of us are set in our ways and have formed habits or addictions to certain substances or routines. Overcoming these habits can be a huge task. Can you imagine drinking coffee every morning for twenty years and then being told to stop? It would be pretty difficult, wouldn't it?

Are there things in your life that could possibly harm you in the future if you don't let go of them? These habits that initially seem harmless later control you. If you are in this boat, seek help before it is too late.

Only the Strong Say "I'm Sorry"

Nothing is more gracious than admitting a fault and making amends. Manipulating or sweeping things under the carpet will only make the situation worse and will come back to haunt you in the end. Being quick to admit your fault is a good attribute to have. Dale Carnegie states in his book *How to Win Friends and Influence People* that it is better to lose an argument than a relationship.

Are you going to let significant relationships slip away because of your pride? Pride is like baggage, so drop it. Admitting you are wrong is not a sign of weakness but of strength. Once you admit your shortcomings, make sure you have thought them through and then have a strategy so as to not repeat them in future. Let your actions speak louder than your words. So pick up the phone, send that e-mail, or schedule a meeting to reconcile with someone today.

Be Excited about You

Have you been to a movie lately that excited you? If you are like me, I then tell all my friends to see the movie, and my enthusiasm and passion influences some of them to see it. Likewise, the sooner you realize that you and only you are your best cheerleader, the more you take responsibility for the signals you send to others about yourself. If you are not excited about your dreams and life, why should anybody else be?

Being Yourself Is a Battle You Never Lose

I believe people often misinterpret the expression "Be yourself." So what does it really mean? Being yourself is being the best you can be at any point in time. In order to be the best, you must know yourself. Your perception of yourself will determine your sphere of influence. In the Bible, Jesus likened his disciples to salt, which I believe is because he knew the importance and power of self-identity. Salt does not only add flavor to food, but it is also an essential nutrient. Low salt levels in people can lead to muscles not contracting, poor blood circulation, and even death. So how would you describe yourself? I tell myself that I am like a precious metal; I add value to people's lives.'"

When you are yourself, your actions are consistent with your values and belief system. Most people fear rejection but if you have to change who you are to be accepted, you are definitely in the wrong relationship.

Being yourself requires honesty, which is a prerequisite for intimacy in relationships. Being yourself is giving what you have and not what you wish you had. You must love yourself completely; love your strengths, and accommodate your weaknesses. You must see yourself as having something to offer. People who conform are not the ones people look to for transformation.

You deserve a place at the table of life. Trying to be something you're not takes more energy, so why try? Your experiences, either positive or negative, are what make you unique.

Whatever Does Not Add Value, Devalues

Athletes know that anything that does not help or enhance their performance must go. And like an athlete, every now and again I take inventory of my life, relationships, and career and sustain or improve the things I have done well and uproot the things that have weighed me down.

Take stock of your life. What is hindering your peak performance? It needs to go, period. No one discovers a tumor in his or her body and saves it as keepsake. If you received a message from your computer saying it had been infected with a virus, the first thing you would do is press the cleanup button. Likewise, whatever does not add value to your life needs to go.

Expect a Little, Give a Lot

How do you feel when your good gestures or actions are not being reciprocated? To be honest, I used to feel disappointed and not appreciated. I believe it is within our nature to expect a returned favor. I was speaking to Mia (my American mom) the other day and she shed some insight on this subject, which I found very helpful. Mia said she always taught her children to do the right things for two reasons; for satisfaction and to always follow their hearts.

An area most of us tend to get very disappointed and even hurt is in our interpersonal relationships. I read a book titled "The 80/20 Principle" by Richard Koch. The principle provided some insight that transformed my thinking when applied to relationships. For example, most of us would hope that if we put in a 100% effort in an endeavor, it would yield a matching return. On the contrary, the 80/20 principle suggests that most things in life do not work that way. The 80/20 principle also known as Pareto principle is named after the Italian economist Vilfredo Pareto who observed in 1906 that 80% of the land in Italy was owned by 20% of the population. This principle is also applicable in modern times. Over 80% of the world's wealth is controlled by the richest 20% of the population (I guess that is why the Occupy Movement is so angry). Over 80% of crimes are committed by 20% of criminals. Richard also adds that the Pareto principle could be 60/40, 70/30, 75/25, or 99/1. This just shows that our efforts are not always proportional to the results we get.

If we apply this principle to our relationships, it means that 20% of the people in your life will bring about 80% of support and satisfaction. Simply put, no one can meet 100% of our needs. So, if we expect the same amount of return as we have invested in others, then we may be disappointed. This means we have to take responsibility to ensure that our unfilled needs are met. This can be achieved by growing your social circle. The Pareto principle suggests that you should enjoy the maximum that you can get from each relationship you are in without destroying it with unmet expectations. An advantage of this viewpoint is that, it helps us reduce our expectation off anyone person or group being everything to us. This reduces disappointments that could occur due to unmet desires. Another benefit is that, it ensures each one of us builds a community of loved ones to support us. I enjoy the outdoors but my wife is more of an indoor person. We try to compromise now and again so that we are both happy. I also take advantage of going outdoors with some of our family friends without my wife feeling short. Likewise in friendships, I have some friends who are introverts while others are social butterflies. I do not try to convert any group to be like the other, I just enjoy each one of them. This has made my interpersonal relationships richer and more rewarding.

The Pareto principle should not be used as an excuse not to patiently love people until the change you expect in them happens. Both parties need to be on the same page when it comes to applying the 80/20 principle in your relationships.

Having a mind frame that people owe you because you have been good to them is setting yourself up for a life of bitterness. In reality there is no guarantee that people will give you back something in return. So it is imperative we build a community that can support us. It is not an easy principle to apply in relationships but it is totally worth it.

Genuine or Fake?

Rolex watches are one of the ten most counterfeited items sold. It takes a trained eye to distinguish between an original and a fake. Can you recognize a genuine person when you meet one? Genuine people are those who don't have it all together but make the most of what they have. They are often happy, confident, and approachable. Superficial people, on the other hand, are usually "show" people; it is all about appearances. They live for other people's approval and try to portray everything as perfect. They may get by fooling others for a while, but the truth finally catches up with them.

Get over it. Everyone has issues they are dealing with in their lives. The difference between genuine and superficial people is that genuine people acknowledge their weaknesses and still live content lives while superficial people try to hide theirs and use them to define the rest of their lives.

We all have areas in our lives we struggle with, but we can seek help rather than sweep them under the rug.

Change with Change or Be Exchanged

I had mixed feelings when we moved to a different neighborhood when I was growing up. I was excited we were moving into a new house, but these feelings faded quickly when I thought about the friends I wouldn't see anymore. I was not sure what our new environment would look like. Would the neighbors be friendly? Would I make new friends? Would the other kids even like me? So many questions flew through my head but very few answers. The thought of how things were going to be different was frightening.

I have come to accept that change is the only constant in this world. I didn't like change because I was uncertain of what it would bring. We all want predictability in our lives to some degree. In my experience, change is an opportunity to get it right, a second chance to redefine and evolve.

Change comes to all of us and is a matter of when, not if. I believe the best way to prepare for change is to enjoy every season of life and leave no room for regrets. There are many things over which we have no control, but we do have a say about our memories. It takes only a moment for reality to become a memory, so make every one of them count.

Before You Dive In, Clarify

At an awesome couple's seminar, presenters Les and Leslie Parrot shared the following situation they had witnessed. In two separate weddings, the ring bearers made funny expressions and growled when they walked down the aisle. They later discovered that the ring bearers thought they were to act like bears. In fact, one of the ring bearers thought he was going to wear a bear suit!

This may sound hilarious, but it drives home a point. People view and interpret things through their beliefs and perspectives, so it is a good idea to see if both parties are on the same page rather than assume they are. Before you dive into an assumption or conclusion, please clarify.

Self-Care versus Selfishness

There is nothing wrong with taking care of yourself. Self-care is helping yourself first so you can be of help to others later while selfishness is helping yourself and not caring what happens to others.

I remember a story about a man who asked his ex-girlfriend to return to him. He told her he missed the way she made him feel. She responded that she was not coming back to him because all he ever talked and cared about was himself.

A good example of self-care is the flight attendants' instructions to put on your oxygen mask before trying to help someone else. In order to help someone else, you need to be whole yourself. You cannot give what you don't have. You need to be healthy first before you can offer help to others. I have been unsuccessful in some of my endeavors, but I have also tasted success. My diverse experiences have equipped me to help others who are going through similar situations.

During tough times, the real you is revealed. Take care of your mental, emotional, and physical health first before trying to help someone else.

When in Rome ...

I worked as a teaching consultant, which required a lot of meetings to prepare for our busy calendar year. During one of our meetings, we were discussing a subject I was really passionate about, but other people volunteered to take lead roles on the project. One of my colleagues was surprised that I did not volunteer to take a lead role. I told her I really wanted to participate but was expecting to be nominated since other people knew I was the man for the job. My colleague was stunned by my explanation, so I had to explain to her that my culture encouraged other people to nominate you for a task, and that volunteering could be mistaken for arrogance. She was kind enough to explain to me that in the American culture volunteering is a sign of passion for something. I have since learned to volunteer rather than wait to be called upon when I have something to offer.

When in Rome behave like the Romans as long as it does not compromise your core values.

Don't Junk the Car Because the Battery Is Dead

One day, someone corrected me rather hurtfully. I had two options—either focus on the message and ignore the criticism or focus on the criticism and ignore the message.

Someone might argue that you can listen to the message and correct the delivery. But in reality, you don't always have the latter option. Many people will speak to you in less than desirable ways, sometimes purposefully, but many times not. A good idea is to put on your filtering ears and listen to the message and not to the extras.

Wear the Shirt, Not the Tag

There is no doubt that people form an impression of you based on how you dress. I have always wondered why a person dresses up so much for an interview even though he or she may never wear those clothes even if they got the job. In *Pretty Woman*, Julia Roberts was treated poorly while shopping because she did not look a certain way. While that may be only a movie, I have experienced the same thing.

The truth is, your appearance matters. People do judge you by your appearance. No wonder people who are in debt still spend heavily on their appearance. They are seeking acceptance from others. It is important that you believe in yourself. Clothes are just enhancements. They should not make or define you. Develop your own style, which means wearing what suits you. Fashion is for the present while style is for life.

I do not believe there is a definitive correlation between dress and character. Some individuals have abused and stereotyped people based on how they were dressed.

I believe you should look your best because you deserve it. But looking good does not mean designer labels. Here is a quick test for you. Will you feel or act any different in a crowd if you are wearing a Ralph Lauren shirt or a shirt from a thrift shop? Really you shouldn't. You are not *what* you wear. You *make* what you wear. In high school, a friend of mine said he was not going to school on an out-of-uniform day because he did not have a brand-name shirt a particular group in school wore.

The truth is, friend, you make what you wear look like a million dollars from the inner beauty that radiates from within you. I also believe you should dress the part. If you want to be the CEO of a Fortune 500 company, you need to start dressing for your future position.

Whatever your status and income level, you can always look like a million dollars when you wear a smile and have a solid belief in yourself that you are worth it.

Inferiority Complex

Every one of us at some point has had to work through a process of discovery. Insecurity is one of the phases you go through in this stage. Some people go through this phase well, as they have learned to accept their weaknesses and to celebrate their strengths. They realize no one is perfect, so they have embraced their uniqueness. Others, however, get stuck in this stage and constantly look to others for reassurance and affirmation to feel complete or balanced. They need people to treat them a particular way in order to feel special.

To be free from the insecurity phase, it is important to get to the root of what is causing you to seek others' approval. An inferiority complex is like filling a basket with water; it never gets full. To solve the problem, you need to line the basket so it can retain water. This is necessary if you want to live a free, happy, and productive life.

Reach Out to Others

I had my turning point regarding making friends after reading Dale Carnegie's book *How To Win Friends and Influence People* where he says, "You make more friends in two months by being interested in others than in two years by expecting others to be interested in you[11]." I learned that relationships are based on what I can give to others, not what I can get from them.

An easy way to connect with people is to give them a genuine compliment. Giving a compliment is so powerful. Besides, whatever you give will come back to you. So, friend, rather than wait for someone to make your day, why don't you make someone else's day? Send that card, make that call, write that letter, give that smile, or say "thank you" or "I'm sorry."

Make someone else's day. By so doing, you will make yours.

Power Reveals Who You Are

Have you met people who move from assertive to aggressive once they have a bit of authority? There are also people who use power to make friends by bending and breaking all the rules. Either way, power shouldn't change you; it should help you accomplish your dreams by empowering other people, not taking advantage of them. If power changes your attitude, it means you were insecure and needed a power drug to make you feel significant.

You add value to your position, your position should not add value to you. Remember the golden words of Walter Winchell, "It pays to be nice to the people you meet on the way up, for they are the same people you meet on the way down".

Be careful how you treat people when climbing the success ladder, you may need them in the future.

Strong Foundation

Have you ever walked around New York with all its magnificent buildings and skyscrapers? The skyscrapers have always gotten my attention because what supports these magnificent buildings is not seen. The strength of the building is its base. To build a skyscraper you need to first dig down before you build up. Likewise, to build a great relationship or career, you must focus first on building a solid foundation.

Effective communication is essential in any healthy relationship. Too many people emphasize attraction, appearance, and career. Please don't get me wrong, those qualities are important, but I believe the most important one is your communication chemistry.

A friend once told me about his sister's marriage. She had a form of cancer that prevented her from being intimate with her husband for over five years. She told him to move on, but he refused and was content being with her. I asked my friend why he thought his brother-in-law stayed and was faithful to her. My friend told me his brother-in-law said it was easy to find a bedmate, but a soul mate and friend was a gift. He had found both, so he was not going to give that up, even for physical intimacy.

In our interpersonal relationships, the foundation will determine the height of our buildings. Great buildings always start from the ground up.

What You Don't Destroy Will Hunt You Down

In history, when people went to conquer an enemy territory, they often killed all the warriors and sadly the women and children. The reason for this was because they feared retaliation from the children once they had grown up and mastered the art of war. Likewise, in our lives we all have some little foxes that could hunt us down if they are not dealt with on time.

Look at world-renowned leaders, religious authorities, and celebrities who moved from grace to grass because of issues they swept under the rug or refused to seek help for when they were younger. They were probably too scared or ashamed to talk about them, but the end result was shame.

Seek help for your issues before it is too late. A tarnished reputation is hard to rebuild, but you can save yourself the pain by seeking assistance early. Speak to counselors, family members, friends, and anyone else who can help you. It is better to humble yourself now and seek help than pay the price of shame and regret when your reputation and those of your loved ones are damaged.

Tempers and Feelings: Yours and Theirs

Put Offenses in Two Boxes

Like it or not, people will always push your buttons knowingly or unknowingly. It may become easy to escape people problems when space travel becomes available for everyone, but until that happens, it is key you learn how to respond to situations and challenges that come your way.

A professor told me he had developed a way of handling issues in the lab while in graduate school that helped him maintain his sanity. He told me to get two boxes, and label the first box "Annoying and Irritating" and the second box "Damaging." Issues related to the first box were to be ignored, and those related to the second box were to be confronted. Remember that an issue in box one may need to be moved to box two and vice versa.

I have since followed his advice, and it has worked very well for me. The glory of a wise person is to overlook an offense.

Capital "No" to Comparison

When you compare yourself with other people, two things can happen. You may feel you are better than others or you feel you are way off the mark. Feeling that you are better than others can make you proud and arrogant while feeling that you fall below others can bring guilt and condemnation. Neither are healthy.

Why are you making any one person your standard? In the land of the blind, a one-eyed man is the king. You need to accept that there will always be people above or below you in all areas. Nobody wins when you compare yourself to others, the key is to be content with who you are and strive to be the best you can be at all times.

Respect Yourself to Be Respected

Have you ever wondered why you do not see a Ferrari advertised on TV? The truth is, it is not made for everyone. The people who buy Ferraris know where to look. Hello! You are not Mr. or Miss Available to everyone. Trying to please everyone but yourself is a recipe for unhappiness. Allowing people to step on you like a doormat is disrespecting yourself. If you do not value yourself, why should anyone else?

Just like the Ferrari is not for everyone, neither are you, so stop trying to satisfy everyone. Your true friends will accept you as you are. It is possible you have not found them yet. Meanwhile, please be yourself. The quickest way to lose friends, in my opinion, is by not recognizing your value. People can make a positive difference in your life, but they cannot make you significant. You are precious just as you are.

Do not be just anybody just to become somebody to everybody. You are a rare gem. Not everyone is worthy of your affection and devotion.

Relax, Think, and Respond

Extroverts have a tendency to have a short fuse, and so they have a tendency to blow up over everything. This can create conflict with the people in their lives, who live in constant tension from watching what they say and do so as not to detonate the extrovert. I know this because I have traveled that path.

One thing that helps is to give a gentle answer and avoid interrupting others when they are expressing themselves. You don't have to give your two cents all the time. In fact, being patient calms quarrels. Think it through rather than feel it through. It could just save you from losing another important person in your life.

Celebrate Those Who Celebrate You

Are you running in a crazy cycle? Have you realized you may be chasing something you cannot have? You keep trying so hard to get the attention of those who ignore you while you take for granted the kindness of those who offer their love freely. It is human nature to chase, that which eludes us and elude that, which chases us. I was a victim of this until I came across the wise saying. "Celebrate those who celebrate you". Surround yourself with people who appreciate you. You won't have to prove a thing to them to feel accepted and you are not on a performance-based relationship with them. Those who celebrate you love you for who you are and not what you are. No wonder it is so easy to be yourself around them. True love is a gift and should never have to be earned. It is a fact of life that people have a tendency to take for granted what they don't work for, but it is also interesting that the best things in life are free. If that's the case, you need to be careful not to take for granted relationships that come easily into your life. My advice, celebrate those who celebrate you.

You Cannot Help a Person Who Is Full

You cannot add any more water to a full glass of water without a spill. Likewise, people who think they know everything—and even know what they do not know—are weights on any team or relationship. They consider their perspectives as the best and consider any other views as average when they do not agree with theirs.

Early recognition of this trait in people will save you time and energy in disconnecting with relationships that have no potential for survival. The Dead Sea does not have any room to mix and so does not create an atmosphere for living organisms to survive. The Dead Sea only receives and does not give. The best help you can give people with this trait is to minimize your contact with them.

Vulnerability Shows You Are Human

I am a firm believer in aiming to be the best you can be and achieving excellence. I also believe that aiming for excellence is a journey, and that some of the greatest experiences you will have on that road is learning from your mistakes.

We all have blind spots, those things other people see in us that we do not see in ourselves. No one is perfect, and when we try to pretend that we are, we come across as insincere. I realized that accepting my vulnerability was actually a sign of strength, not weakness. I am now comfortable enough with myself to embrace the good, the bad, and the ugly.

Your vulnerability, when given expression, is a gift to yourself, which allows you to grow, love, and be loved.

It's Okay to Be Angry

I repeat, it's okay to be angry. It's okay to express yourself as long as you do not point fingers or threaten anyone. It's *not* okay to sweep your feelings under the carpet or be a doormat just to keep the peace and make everyone else happy.

Expressing anger is different from being hostile or vindictive. Take responsibility for your feelings. Healthy relationships allow people to express themselves without fearing the loss of affection or attention.

Hang Around People You Want to Be Like

Iron sharpens iron, so one person sharpens another, Proverbs 27:17, New International Version. So to be wise, you need to keep company with wise people. I was not doing as well as I expected despite all my hard work in my first year of college, so I decided to seek the counsel of people who worked hard and had positive results to show for it. I shadowed them and observed their study habits. I guess you can predict the rest of the story—my grades improved significantly.

It is okay to admire the qualities of others and aspire to acquire them without losing yourself. The quickest way to improve is to hang around people whose qualities you aspire to develop, and when you cannot physically be with them, read their books.

A Car Without Brakes Is a Moving Casket

We all have people in our lives who push our innermost buttons. But we can take back the power we have given them by seeing them in another light. They are simply teaching us patience. So when they push our buttons, we should now say, "Welcome to Patience 101."

No matter your situation or status in life, your ability to restrain yourself is one of your greatest assets. Power loses significance if you have no control over it. The only person you have the right to control is yourself, and that's one right you don't want to give away. Many lives and dreams have been shattered because someone could not delay an action or just keep quiet.

Practice self-control today. Practice can become permanent.

Don't Judge a Book By Its Cover, Open It

I remember watching *Britain's Got Talent* when it was Susan Boyles's turn to sing. The facial expressions of the judges and those in the audience were less than encouraging. It seemed everyone was waiting to have a good laugh. Her song was dead on arrival based on people's perception of her. But then Susan opened her mouth, and that was it. The world was wrong. She was judged by her age, appearance, and supposed lack of potential, but she got her opportunity and made history.

Likewise, do not let other people limit you by what they think of you. You can be anything you want to be. Susan took a bold step and followed her dream despite the odds. Guess who is having the time of her life now?

The Greatest Love of All

I saw this on a placard at cell group the other night, "I tell myself, 'I love me, God loves me, and if you don't love me, it is your problem. One of the greatest commandments of the Bible is to love your neighbor as you love yourself. Loving yourself is not being self-absorbed or self-focused. Rather, it is being the best you can be so you can be of help to others. You cannot truly love other people without loving yourself first. To clarify, I do not mean being conceited or selfish but rather understanding that you are a person of significance and that you matter in this world. You are a voice, not an echo; a victor, not a victim. Yes, life may have been unkind to you, but you can choose to see the light at the end of the tunnel.

Treat people the way you wish to be treated. You can only control your actions, not those of others. Some people will respond positively to your kind gestures, others may be suspicious and even reject them. The key to contentment is your capacity to love and knowing that the problem is not with you.

Loving yourself requires taking daily steps that create a good future for you and your loved ones.

Seek to Understand Than Be Understood

I have a fourteen-month-old son who always wants to grab everything in sight. He does not have a clue as to what is important. To him, everything is meant to be ripped apart and explored, and he has torn up many important documents. Though I was upset, I knew he did not know any better at that age, which helped me to not get angry with him.

Being understanding does not mean we don't feel pain, but rather the information we have makes us handle the experience without becoming bitter. In our personal lives, having the right information is vital to put things in perspective, and that can make a big difference between understanding and overreacting or being insensitive.

The Danger of a Single-Sided Story

I watched an online TED talk where the speaker, Chimamanda Adichie, spoke about the danger of a single-sided story. A single-sided story only portrays one side of a story. It is not a balanced story. In my first year of graduate school, I was asked by one of my students if we had televisions in Africa. Though I was slightly irritated by the question, I knew he was sincerely ignorant and wanted to learn. His question made me realize how the biased view of the media had shaped his opinions and beliefs. The media has achieved a lot of great things for the world, but many people, nations, and establishments have become victims of the single-sided story.

I must say I too am guilty of believing single-sided stories and have now learned to question things I hear and read about. I am always interested in diverse opinions from other knowledgable sources. This has helped me make informed decisions in my personal and professional life.

The Truth Is Liberating

I was watching a Joel Osteen broadcast where he shared a very interesting analysis. He said that 25 percent of people will always like you, 25 percent of people will dislike you no matter what you do, and that our attitude determines the remaining 50 percent. Joel said you can either move that remaining 50 percent into the "like" or "dislike" column.

This analysis has saved me a lot of stress, as it has enabled me to identify those I have gone over and above trying please but with little success. Their attitudes never changed toward me regardless of my overtures toward them. This analysis helped me release them in my mind, and I said good-bye to them.

It was also comforting to know that at least 25 percent of people will like me no matter what (friends and family). For some, that percentage is all they need. The big question for me is, What am I going to do with the remaining 50 percent? I hope my actions and attitude are not unconsciously moving me toward the "dislike" column.

To become a person of influence, learning how to get along with others is important. Dale Carnegie's book *How To Win Friends and Influence People* is a great place to start.

Your "Weather Signal"

When it is cold, people put on a coat to keep warm. When it is hot, people put on light clothing. When the weather is pleasant, people just want to relax outside and have a good time.

Do you realize that each of us send messages to others based on our gestures, body language, attitude, etc.? When people try to connect with us, our verbal and nonverbal responses transmit our "weather signal," which determines how they respond to and interact with us.

A smile, eye contact, and a warm handshake send positive signals. With a pleasant weather signal, people are comfortable with us, and that's when connections are established. What is your weather signal like?

Before Complaining, Ask

I had a tough but lovely choir director when I was growing up. We practiced for six hours at a stretch. On one occasion, she sipped some water and then handed it to one of the choristers. Seeing the expression on everyone's faces, she explained that she gave the chorister water because she had asked, not because she was being partial.

I have encountered scenarios where I have felt that some people in my life received preferential treatment, but then I remember that rehearsal story, which helps me put things in perspective. I can ask, too.

Love, a Leadership Prerequisite

Jimi Hendrix said, "When the power of love overcomes the love of power, the world will know peace." So are you a leader, or do you want to be one? There is one requirement that is absolutely essential: You must be a people person. You cannot lead people if you do not care about them.

It is possible to boss others around and get some work done, but that is not effective leadership. Some leaders have more people skills than others, but you can learn them. Being a leader carries a lot of responsibility, including having a genuine interest in others. People will see through you and your actions and will know whether you really care about them or if you are just using them for your own ego trip.

To be an effective leader, you must be patient and be a good listener. It is more about what you give rather than what you receive. Leadership is not about you but about those you are leading.

First Impressions

Whatever it takes, friends, learn not to pass judgment on first impressions. This is a must-have quality in order to get along with others. We live in a day and age where people form opinions within seconds of seeing and speaking with someone. Once made, these opinions are hard to change.

Meeting a person after they have had a bad day or a great day will tell a different story about them. In order to get a true picture of a person, we must see beyond our first impression. We all want to be given second chances, so let us give them to others.

Make Your Personality Work for You

This is often a tricky subject, with diverse perspectives and materials. In order to make your personality work for you, it is important to understand how your personality works with others. This will help reduce countless, avoidable conflicts.

A Nigerian prayer says it is important you do not make your wife your girlfriend or make your girlfriend your wife. I know this may sound crazy, but here is the interpretation. Some relationships are better left as friendships rather than trying to make them romantic. Some personalities naturally work well together while others don't. Some people say opposites attract, but that's not necessarily true.

Take some time to think about the relationships that have had the biggest impact on your life. Look at the connections you have made that left you damaged or deeply hurt. What do the positive connections have in common? What do the negative connections have in common? You will notice you have a certain feeling when you think about a particular person or when you are in their presence. Do some research by visiting websites, such as Meyer-Briggs and Personality Plus, that provide information about different personalities, their characteristics, and how you can maximize your communication by adapting to each personality style. While it is good to have an understanding of who you are, it should never be an excuse to justify some peculiar traits. A well-rounded person should have some characteristics from each of the different personality styles.

One of the ways to be a person people are comfortable with is to learn how to reach out to people you normally clash with. You can be someone who sees the best in others and develops excellent interpersonal skills. A Nigerian proverb says, "Kiki konsore," which means, "Saying hello to a stranger doesn't mean you are friends." It is a great way to make a connection, though.

What Are You Wearing?

A middle-aged lady walked past me in the mall the other day. I liked the fragrance she was wearing. Although it was modest, it left an impression after she passed. I then noticed I was unconsciously attributing her fragrance to her personality, although I had no basis for my assessment besides the fragrance she was wearing. My perception could have been far from reality, but for the sake of make-believe, I assumed she was a nice person.

Someone complimented me on my fragrance at a gas station one time. The lady wanted to know the name of it so she could recommend it to her husband. It has since occurred to me that the fragrance people wear can be likened to their personalities and thus affects people's perception of them.

Your character and attitude are the fragrance you wear, and they can attract or repel others. Wearing a smile and having a positive attitude is the best fragrance you can wear. The good news is they are free. It takes more energy to frown than to smile.

Apology Accepted on Behavioral Change

I have met several people who apologize for a wrongdoing but do not back it up with their actions. They are very quick to say, "I'm sorry," but also swift to repeat the same offense. This really frustrates me because the apology comes across as insincere. Some people's way of showing remorse is only through their actions while others admit their remorse verbally and then back it up with their behavior. To establish meaningful relationships, it is important that we take responsibility for our deeds. People who never admit their shortcomings are often defensive and critical of everyone but themselves. This attitude is a turnoff and burns many bridges.

The best apologies are the ones that are accompanied with a change.

You Determine What Gets to You

Life is filled with people who constantly burst our bubbles. I remember when a friend of mine accidentally stepped on my foot. He was sorry for his action, but the pain was still severe.

Likewise, many hurts are not intentional, but that's not an instant remedy for the discomfort they cause us. After getting hurt many times, I decided I had to choose to either meditate on the bad experiences and relive them or simply let them go.

Focusing on a problem makes it look bigger than it actually is. We cannot control other people's actions, but we can exercise absolute power over ourselves. Offenses will surely come, and there is nothing we can do about that. But the good news is we can choose our response.

References

1. Elizabeth Dunn, Lara B. Aknin, Michael I. Norton. *Spending Money on Others Promotes Happiness.* Science 21 March 2008: 1687-1688
2. Massachuttes Insitute of Technology. *Brain and Cognitive Science.* Available online at http://web.mit.edu/~bcs/newsevents/bcsnews.shtml . Last accessed July 22, 2012.
3. Merriam –Webster. Defintion of Poison. Available online at https://mail.google.com/mail/#search/citations/13911623d3cefc0e . Last accessed August 25, 2012
4. Celine Dion, *Because you loved me.* Columbia, Epic. February 19, 1996. Compact disc
5. Search Quotes. *Lee Segall Quotes.* Available online at http://www.searchquotes.com/search/Lee_Segall/. Last accessed August 25, 2012.
6. Council for Exceptional Children. *Giftedness and the Gifted: What's It all About. Available online at* http://www.cec.sped.org/AM/Template.cfm?Section=Gifts_and_Talents&Template=/TaggedPage/TaggedPageDisplay.cfm&TPLID=37&ContentID=5628. Last accessed August 25, 2012.
7. Merriam-Webster. *Definition of Grace.* Available online at http://www.merriam-webster.com/dictionary/grace . Last accessed August 25, 2012.
8. Search Quotes. *John Maxwell Quotes.* Available online at http://www.searchquotes.com/quotation/A_man_must_be_big_enough_to_admit_his_mistakes,_smart_enough_to_profit_from_them,_and_strong_enough_/150310/ . Last accessed August 25, 2012.
9. George Matthew Adams. BrainyQuote.com, Xplore Inc, 2012. http://www.brainyquote.com/quotes/quotes/g/georgematt390925.html, accessed August 29, 2012.

10. John C. Maxwell. BrainyQuote.com, Xplore Inc, 2012. http://www.brainyquote.com/quotes/quotes/j/johncmaxw391398.html, accessed August 29, 2012.
11. Dale Carnegie. BrainyQuote.com, Xplore Inc, 2012. http://www.brainyquote.com/quotes/quotes/d/dalecarneg103476.html, accessed August 29, 2012.

CPSIA information can be obtained at www.ICGtesting.com
Printed in the USA
BVOW021150010413

316976BV00003B/8/P